art
activities
for
the
very
young

from 3

to 6 years

F. Louis Hoover

HEAD, DEPARTMENT OF ART
Illinois State Normal
University
Normal, Illinois

&

Editor
Arts and Activities
magazine

DAVIS
PUBLICATIONS,
INC.
Worcester,
Massachusetts

Library of Congress
Catalog Card Number: 61-11263

Copyright 1961

by DAVIS PUBLICATIONS, INC.

Worcester, Massachusetts

Second Printing—1963

Table of Contents

Acknowledgments

There are many to whom I am indebted for assistance in preparing this book. Special thanks to all the very young children with whom I have had the pleasure of working over a period of many years and who permitted me to share the excitement and satisfaction of their creative art experiences.

One of the most valuable helps has been the opportunity to visit kindergartens in various parts of the country and to talk and work with outstanding kindergarten teachers. I am especially grateful to Peggy McIntyre whose unique understanding of the role of the arts in early childhood education made her kindergarten room at Illinois State Normal University a unique laboratory for carrying out many ideas in working with four- and five-year-olds.

Sincere thanks to the publishers of Arts and Activities *magazine who graciously consented to the use of material which previously had been included in articles prepared especially for that publication. I also wish to express appreciation to the public schools which supplied me with photographs for illustrative material.*

My deepest gratitude goes to my wife whose constant encouragement and faith made this book possible.

F. L. H.

Helpful Hints

1 *Child art has a distinct charm of its own.   The most successful examples of child art are honest, forthright expressions of the child's world as he feels it and understands it to be.*

2 *Young children do not draw things the way they look to adults.   They draw and paint their own world in their own way.   It is different from an adult's world. It is a young child's world.*

3 *The very young child is not concerned with using color imitatively as it appears in nature.   A cat may be green or a house purple.   This element of fantasy is consistent with the exciting impossibilities of fairy tales.   So we understand and enjoy this element of fantasy in child art.*

4 *It is almost impossible to fake an enjoyment of child art.   We must genuinely enjoy child art in order to encourage its growth and development successfully.*

5 *Through our actions and attitudes, we convince young children that we have complete faith in their ability to express their own ideas in their own way.*

6 *There is no place in creative art expression for patterns, stereotyped cutouts, Hectographed outlines or coloring books.   They block the development of a young child's creative powers.*

7 *Every art activity must be a creative experience which requires original thinking, planning and doing.*

8 *Young children are proud of their creative art expressions and need our approval for further development.   We praise their efforts and proudly display their work in the home and at school.*

9 *We never draw for a young child in order to "help him".   This retards his creative development and makes him dissatisfied with his own efforts.*

10 *We never try to hurry or push a child who is still in the scribble stage.   This only slows his progress toward the next developmental stage.*

11 *Children do not create at the same rate of speed. Some are slower than others in developing original ideas. Unfinished work should be left where a child may work on it when he wishes to do so.*

12 *By referring to children's scribbles as* designs, *the young child has a ready answer to the inevitable question by adults: "What is it?" The young child answers with a toss of his head, "It's a design."*

13 *We encourage children to verbalize about their paintings and other art expressions. Talking about their work seems to give them greater confidence—especially when the listener shows a genuine interest in the child's work.*

14 *Young children determine the size of things they draw and paint by the importance they wish to give them. A flower may be larger than a building because the flower is more important to the child. This is completely logical to the child—as it is to many professional artists.*

15 *The timid child sometimes tends to draw and paint in a small, tight manner. Through praise and encouragement we stimulate children to work big, to think big and to act big. This is our opportunity to find the right key which will unlock the door to the child's inner self—to free him from tensions—to release a joyous outpouring of creative expression.*

16 *Yes, all young children have the potential for creative expression. It is the responsibility of parents and teachers to provide opportunities for this potential to develop as fully as possible. It is not the child's fault if this does not happen. It is ours.*

Art activities should always be creative experiences in which the young child solves a problem in his own unique way.

To The Parent

Every child has creative ability. To be sure, some are blessed with more creativity than others, but all children can find pleasure and satisfaction through art activities—if they have the right kind of guidance and encouragement.

It is not difficult to set free the creative spirit in a young child. Many parents and teachers learn to do this effectively. But it is also easy for well-meaning but uninformed adults to stifle a young child's creativity so that it becomes difficult if not impossible for him to find satisfaction through art activities.

We used to think there was time enough to develop creativeness in children after they entered the 1st grade at school. Now we know this is not true. The time to begin is when a child first begins to scribble with a crayon and builds his first tower of blocks *at home*. The manner in which parents respond to these early creative interests affects the entire development of a child's creative powers.

We are not speaking of the child as a potential artist. Relatively few choose art as a career. We are concerned here with the development of people who think imaginatively, who have original ideas and welcome opportunities to put them into action. America needs effective leaders—not more passive followers.

Creative art experiences are among the most effective devices known for developing this creative potential.

What can parents do who want to develop the latent creativity in their children? They can encourage all kinds of experiences which rely upon original thinking and doing.

But we must be willing to start at the beginning. We can't rush creative development. It is a slow process. It must be allowed to grow and flourish at its own rate of speed. Our responsibility as parents is to recognize the importance of the creative act and to encourage it in every way possible.

The first time a baby puts his foot against a solid object and pushes himself forward a few inches, we recognize and applaud the act as a milestone in the process of learning to walk. In a similar way, a young child's scribbles are an important first step toward creative expression in art. Young children should receive warm praise for producing these first scribbles and be given encouragement for further efforts.

The important point is that all children pass through many stages in their creative development—awkward, sometimes meaningless-looking stages, before they are ready to express and interpret their world in a way in which it will be recognizable and meaningful to adults.

Parents should take an active interest in the creative expressions of their children. They should praise their efforts and provide encouragement in the development of original ideas.

7

Young children should never be pushed or hurried to *draw something*. Such pressures only make them feel inadequate and frustrated. In an attempt to be helpful, sometimes an adult will help a child draw or "correct" his early efforts. The child's natural reaction is that apparently we don't like what he can draw by himself so he puts his hands behind his back and says, "I can't draw. You do it." Then the well-meaning adult sometimes says, "Oh, it's easy. Let me show you how." And he proceeds to draw some trick stereotype of a cat or dog or a person. The young child thinks this is wonderful. It is all very pleasant and everyone seems happy—until we say, "Now, *you* draw something for me." The response is the inevitable: "I can't draw. You show me first." This goes on and on, with thousands of boys and girls completely convinced that they can not think for themselves or draw for themselves unless first they are told what to do or an adult draws something for them to copy.

Color books and adult drawn patterns never will produce young citizens who have inventive minds and the ability to think and do for themselves. Activities must be *creative* experiences which require *original* thinking and planning. Every art activity must be a new adventure.

Can you, a parent with little or no art training, help to develop the potential creativity in your young child in your own home? Of course you can. You will need three basic ingredients for success: a sympathetic and understanding attitude toward child art, a bit of working space and some art materials.

Attitude

If you are not familiar with child art, a typical scribble drawing by a young child may make you feel a bit uneasy. You don't know quite what to say and the whole thing is a bit embarrassing. So you laugh and say, "What is it?"

There, you have already made two mistakes. First we never laugh at a child's sincere effort to do anything. Remember how sensitive we are about things *we* are learning to do. Second, we don't ask, "What is it?" In all probability it isn't anything but some happy lines running around the paper. But the child is at a loss to

know how to answer our question and he quickly gets the idea that we aren't very understanding of his efforts. If we persist in asking such questions, children may find it simpler not to draw at all and then the problem won't come up again. This may result in a person who is fearful of making decisions, of making choices, of seeking to solve a problem, of going into action. It will be easier to wait for the other fellow to "do something about it."

Perhaps you have never seen many examples of creative work by young children. Let me tell you what it is like.

Child art is delightful. It is free and exuberant and unafraid. Sometimes it gets rather messy. But over a period of time the child grows in his ability to express his ideas. With encouragement and guidance, his art expressions become exciting revelations of his innermost thoughts, his feelings and his reactions to the world he lives in.

Professional artists often make special efforts to see exhibitions of child art. They marvel at the extraordinary power of children to see—to express in a very personal and honest way— their world as *they* see it—as *they* feel it—as *they* know it to be. It is difficult for the adult, professional artist to achieve these characteristics in his own work. He envies this seemingly natural ability in children.

Of course those first scribbles are meaningless—as far as subject content is concerned. But there is always something we can say about them to give that all-important encouragement. "What a beautiful red line. I like red too. How strong your muscles are to make the line so big and bright."

Does that sound silly? Try it. Watch the eyes of your child as you smile and praise his work.

It is especially exciting when your child first begins to draw simple symbols which represent people and animals and trees and flowers and cars and airplanes. Instead of asking, "What is it?", suggest that he tell you about his picture. And now the marvelous imagination of the child comes pouring out. No matter that obviously he had not planned one-tenth of what he tells you when he first made the drawing. Encourage his fantastic stories. Enjoy

Children should have a special place at home where they can keep their art materials. They are taught to keep supplies in good order and to put them away after use.

them with him. *Now* you are really helping to develop his creative powers. *Now* you are helping him discover his true self. Because the imagination, like a muscle, needs lots of exercise.

Yes, you have to genuinely enjoy child art. And you must convince your child that you sincerely like his art expressions. You like it because it is *his* art expression and it is different from that of *any other child*. Indeed, it is the uniqueness of any work of art which contributes to its greatness. So you take time to talk about his work with him and you put it up on the wall to give it all the recognition you can. You want him to know that you are proud of it—and him.

As you begin to show your child how to use some of the materials and processes described in this book, you are careful not to indicate how you think the final product will look. Remember it will be *his* idea—not yours. That is the creative experience and it must be entirely the child's own idea. But you do help him learn how to handle tools and materials in order that he may express his ideas more effectively.

Encourage your child to take some of his art work to school. Kindergarten teachers are delighted when parents encourage creative art activities in the home.

Space

Some art activities are a bit messy, but parents who are seriously interested in providing art experiences for their children accept this as part of the price. The kitchen linoleum is not difficult to clean and it is practical for painting and pasting activities. Or you can saw off the legs of a second-hand library table to a height of about 22 inches. Established in one corner of the living room, your youngster can have an *art center* of his own. A sheet of oil cloth or newspapers will protect the floor. Of course it is ideal if your child has a room of his own. Use a couple of wooden boxes for storing art materials. Let him organize his materials and expect him to keep them in order at all times.

As mentioned earlier, it is important that children's art expressions be prominently displayed. A bulletin board in the child's room is excellent for this purpose since items can be easily changed. And don't forget to bring in your friends—as well as his—to see his latest achievements. Guaranteed to pay dividends.

Materials

Don't expect to carry on a successful program of art activities at home with just a box of crayons and a few sheets of typing paper. A

9

good supply of art materials won't cost as much as the swing set out in the yard. Total costs will depend entirely upon how varied and ambitious a program you desire.

With increasing interest in art as a leisure time activity for adults, most communities today have stores which stock art supplies. You may have to do a bit of detective work, but there should be one in your area. There may have to be a bit of substituting occasionally, but here's where your own imagination and inventiveness can come into play.

You want your child to paint on large 18″ x 24″ paper. Don't waste your money and his time on small sheets. This merely cramps his style and encourages him to think small. Unprinted newsprint is the least expensive paper for painting. If you can't find a source for purchasing it by the sheet or pad of sheets, try buying ends of rolls of newsprint from your local newspaper and cut it to size yourself. They can't use the ends of rolls and will be happy to sell them cheaply. Manila paper is a bit more expensive but it has a good surface for painting. If the budget is limited encourage your young artist to paint on the daily newspaper. The classified ad section provides an interesting texture for paintings.

For paint, there are boxes of pre-mixed tempera paints in jars. Or you can purchase one pound cans of dry powder paint that you mix with water. Make up small amounts of several colors in a muffin tray. Quite economical.

Try to find long handled, stiff bristled brushes for painting. If these are not available, get small varnish brushes at your variety store. I mentioned these materials in particular because they are basic. Probably more children enjoy painting than any other type of creative art activity.

This is just to get your program off to a good start. As you read about other activities in this book you will discover that many of the items will be found in your home. Others can be located somewhere between the lumber yard and the junk pile.

And don't forget one last important item: dad's old shirt. Cut off the sleeves and your child has a perfect artist's smock. Not only does it help to dramatize the activity but it also saves mother a lot of washing.

Parents should find opportunities to display child art in the home and to show it to their friends. This pays dividends in future creative production.

To The Teacher

There should be adequate space in the kindergarten room for art materials where children can reach them and help to keep them in order.

Older children sometimes find it difficult to lose themselves in creative art experiences. They become unduly shy about their creative abilities and are reluctant to reveal their own original ideas in visual form.

Not so with very young children. They are honest and forthright in their art expressions. How eagerly they respond to suggestions. How they revel in the challenge of new materials and astonish us with the rapidity in which they learn to manipulate them. With no fears or inhibitions regarding their creative abilities, they draw and paint and model their innermost feelings joyfully and with complete freedom.

It is the kindergarten teacher's responsibility to make good use of this creative energy, to encourage its development in every possible way. That is why such a large portion of the kindergarten budget is allocated to the purchase of art materials. That is why every art activity should be a *creative* experience for the child.

There is no room in the art program for patterns, stereotyped cutouts and Hectographed outlines. The sooner these are discarded from a teacher's file the better. Young teachers should never collect them. The creative spirit of too many children has been permanently crippled by activities which required no original thinking and relied upon adult drawn clichés. From the first day of school, children should take it for granted that whatever they produce with art materials will reflect their own thinking, their own feelings, their own seeing.

Each child's work will look different from that of any other child. Since no two children are alike, their art expressions will be unique. And it is this uniqueness—this quality of *differentness*—which gives child art one of its deepest values.

A successful kindergarten art program does not just happen. It is a planned program of experiences using a wide variety of materials. And it assumes daily participation on the part of *all* the children.

Sinks should be installed at heights suitable for very young children. Paints and brushes are kept near the sink for easy mixing and cleanup.

Merely having art materials available is not enough. Programs which leave all choices to the children often fail because a child who feels insecure hesitates to explore a material with which he is unfamiliar. It is the teacher's responsibility to plan activities—to organize the presentation of a new material or process—so that all the children will look forward with eagerness to this portion of the daily schedule.

There are two different times during the day when kindergartners should have an opportunity to work with art materials. First is the organized period of time when art is a group activity. This is sometimes planned as the first activity of the day so that when the children come into the room appropriate art materials are out on tables and arranged for their use. It is at this time that the teacher may discuss with the children a new material or demonstrate a new process. The length of this activity period will vary depending upon its complexity and whether all the children will participate at one time or take turns by groups. Usually the time will average 30 to 40 minutes including cleanup.

The second time during the day in which children should have an opportunity to work with art materials is during *free* time. Several types of art materials should be available for use by children who are especially interested and who desire more opportunities to work with them.

During the group activity period, art activities should be carried on in an atmosphere of happy invention. It is a time of exploration—not only of materials but of ourselves. We seek out new ideas, we become aware of new feelings, new sensations, and discover new ways in which these can be expressed with our materials.

Children are encouraged to talk about their paintings during sharing time. They make up stories about their pictures and talk about ideas they have for future paintings.

But we also begin to learn new disciplines. These disciplines apply not only to the activity at hand such as the care of tools and equipment, but also how to take turns, how to share materials and respect the work of others.

Usually the teacher finds that her children are at various stages of development relative to their ability to work with materials and to express their ideas effectively. In most kindergarten groups it is not unusual to find a few children who still are in the scribble stage, a large number in the symbolic stage and some in the representational stage. This fact points up the importance of emphasizing to the children that each of us has his own way of working with materials, that each child's work will be different from that of his neighbor and that we, the teacher, will enjoy each child's work equally well. About this we must be sincere and prove it through our actions.

With such a wide variety of art expressions occurring within the group, how do we evaluate the work of kindergartners? There are no valid objective tests for measuring the success of child art. Our primary aim is to produce personal satisfactions within the child through creative expression. We hope that he will find so much pleasure through creative art experiences that he will look forward to future opportunities for using his creative powers. We want him to enjoy original thinking and planning and to have confidence in his ability to express himself effectively with art materials. If you are not sure you are accomplishing these objectives, begin watching the faces of your children more than you do their products. Their eyes will answer your question.

It is recommended that teachers provide some type of folder in which the work of each child can be kept. Each example should be dated so that over a period of time teachers and parents may see how a child is progressing in terms of his past performance.

Some parents may not have a background of understandings necessary for appreciating creative work by young children. They are impatient during the scribble stage and are anxious for their children to draw and paint recognizable forms. The teacher should find opportunities at PTA and other parent meetings to explain how children develop in their ability to express themselves creatively. Parents should be informed of the dangers of patterns and color books so that they will encourage children to carry on art activities at home which will be consistent with the school program. Most parents are eager to cooperate in providing sound art experiences in the home *if* they know how to go about it.

A period of time for cleanup is planned as a basic part of the activity period. Large sponges are accessible to children at all times to wash up spots of paint and paste from tables and floor.

Equipping the Room

Fortunately, most kindergarten rooms are ideal for carrying on art activities. They are relatively large in size, have sinks and low work tables.

It is important that there be sufficient storage cabinets for art materials. These should be designed so that children may assist in getting out materials and putting them away. There should be deep shelves for holding 18" x 24" paper and facilities for storing art work in progress.

A 50-pound metal garbage can with tight fitting lid is suitable for keeping clay moist.

New buildings usually provide adequate bulletin board space for displaying children's work. Older buildings sometimes have an excess of chalkboards which can be converted into bulletin boards by covering them with Celotex or some other type of wallboard.

Two or three double easels equipped with racks for holding jars of paint are nice to have, but they are sometimes more decorative than useful since most of our painting is done on the floor.

The floor should be covered with a good quality of tile so that it may be cleaned with a minimum of effort.

And don't forget to find a good location for your *treasure chest* of scrap materials. As an expert scavenger you will be on the lookout for such items as small cardboard boxes, spools, cotton, feathers, etc. The children can also bring contributions from home.

The best place to paint is on the floor. Don't hesitate to push back tables and chairs for either individual or group painting projects.

Children as Helpers

It is all very well to spend time in organizing art materials before children come into the room, and most kindergarten teachers find it necessary to tidy up the room at the close of the day. But we are not good teachers if we spend hours in cleaning up and putting away materials which the children could and should be expected to do as part of their daily routine. If children are permitted to leave a mess just because they want to work up to the last minute, we are doing them no favor. In fact, we are teaching them poor work habits which will be difficult for parents and future teachers to change. Even though it shortens an already too brief work period, we must leave sufficient time for children to clean up. It is an important part of their education. Large sponges are kept handy which the *sponge brigade* can moisten to wipe up paste and spilled paint from tables and floors. A broom should be available for quick sweep-ups after paper cutting and tearing activities.

Children will take better care of materials and equipment if they are taught where they belong and time is allowed for cleanup committees to see that each is put back in its correct place. Of course it takes a bit longer than for you to do it, but the children are learning to associate good work habits with their art experiences. This is another score for the quality of your art program.

Mothers become fussy when Susan comes home with paint on her new dress. So we require each child to have a smock and see that he wears it whenever he works with materials which may stain or soil clothes. Most teachers seem to prefer the old standard: one of dad's old shirts with the sleeves cut short. Put on backwards and buttoned, it makes a perfect coverall.

Displaying Child Art

Kindergartners love the art work they produce and are the first to admit it. "Come see my work." "Look what I've painted." "Will you put mine up on the wall today?" "It's my turn to tell about my painting."

Even if there is a danger that the room will look a bit cluttered, we put up children's art work until the space is all gone. The children enjoy living among their own art expressions. And when visitors drop in, they can see that important things are going on.

How sad it is to visit neat but dreary kindergarten rooms with tidy little 9″ x 12″ pictures neatly mounted on colored construction papers and lost in the expanse of big bulletin boards.

Children enjoy seeing their work on display. And this encouragement is more important than a sterile kind of tidiness. Use all your space. You may even wish to stretch a wire or two across the room to give more drying space. But how proud we are to have to duck under *our* painting to get to our desk.

Displaying kindergarten work in the school corridor gives further recognition and adds stimulation to the project. But be careful not to choose only the most mature and advanced work. Remember, we are not comparing the work of one child with that of another. We are anxious for each child to know the satisfaction that comes from creative expression. Each child should have his turn in being represented in our displays and exhibits.

Use bulletin boards in the classroom for displaying child art. Change exhibits often so that all children are represented frequently.

ART SUPPLIES

for 1 year/class of 24 children

Item	Description	Amount
BRUSHES		
Paste brushes	short, stiff bristle	24
Painting brushes	$\frac{1}{4}$″ wide, long handled, stiff bristles	18
	$\frac{1}{2}$″ wide, long handled, stiff bristles	18
	water-color brushes, medium size, soft bristles	24
CLAY	water-base, moist, 25 lb. plastic bags	8 bags
CRAYONS	8 color boxes of wax crayons	24 boxes
FASTENERS	brass paper fasteners, 100 per box, 1″ long	4 boxes
FINGER PAINT	1 pint jars, ready mixed	
	red	6 jars
	blue	6 jars
	black	6 jars
	brown	6 jars
	or mix your own	
GLUE	Elmers (or equal) $\frac{1}{2}$ pint squeeze bottle	1 bottle
	fast drying airplane cement in small tubes	24 tubes
MUSLIN	26″ wide, unbleached	24 yards
NAILS	$1\frac{1}{4}$″ long	3 pounds
NEEDLES	tapestry (large eye, blunt point)	24
PAINT	1 lb. cans powder paint	
	red	1 dozen cans
	blue	1 dozen cans
	yellow	1 dozen cans
	green	1 dozen cans
	orange	1 dozen cans
	purple	1 dozen cans
	magenta	1 dozen cans
	turquoise	1 dozen cans
	brown	1 dozen cans
	flesh	1 dozen cans
	black	1 dozen cans
	white	1 dozen cans
PAPER	newsprint, 18″ x 24″	5 packages
	500 sheets per package	
	manila, 18″ x 24″	2 packages
	500 sheets per package	
	manila, 12″ x 18″	4 packages
	500 sheets per package	

P A P E R (contd.)	colored construction	10 packages
	12″ x 18″ assorted packages	
	50 sheets to package	
	roll of white wrapping paper	1 roll
	36″ wide, for murals, backgrounds, etc.	
	finger paint paper, 16″ x 20″	200 sheets
	or	
	14″ x 75″ roll white glazed shelf paper	4 rolls
P A S T E	1 quart jar library paste	2 quarts
R U G Y A R N	¼″ diameter cotton rug yarn	
	for weaving	
	black	4 skeins
	white	4 skeins
	red	4 skeins
	blue	4 skeins
	brown	4 skeins
	beige	4 skeins
	green	4 skeins
	turquoise	4 skeins
S C I S S O R S	4″ blunt points	24
	4″ medium points	6
S T A R C H	1 quart, liquid prepared	2 quarts

*One of the most important sources of materials
is the box of scrap materials. Children should be encouraged
to bring items from home and share them with their classmates.*

Drawing

MATERIALS:
12" x 18" drawing paper
colored crayons

A child's first drawings are his first steps in learning a new language of expression. His efforts will not be understood by the average person any more than his first attempts in speech, but they should receive the same encouragement and praise.

Beginning with the scribble stage, most children seem to follow a similar developmental sequence in learning to draw. However, the particular stage of development on entering kindergarten may vary greatly. The child who has never been given drawing materials or encouraged to use them at home may still be in the scribble stage. Other children from the first day will produce recognizable symbols and be eager to give explanations or tell stories about them. It is important, therefore, that parents and kindergarten teachers understand the various stages the child goes through in learning to draw.

When the young child is first given crayons and paper he learns that by pressing the crayons to the paper he can make marks. It is a pleasurable activity and he happily fills one sheet after another with meaningless scribbles. If his attention is distracted, his hands may continue their uncontrolled activity with lines swinging here and there, on the paper and now off the paper completely. *This is the first step* in learning to draw and his efforts should be highly praised.

"What strong, happy lines you are making."

"I like the way you swing your lines clear across the paper."

A critical remark at this point may well discourage future efforts. Don't try to hurry him into representational drawing. This will come in time.

The child gradually becomes conscious of the fact that he can control the direction of his lines.

A young child's first efforts at drawing are meaningless scribbles. This is an important first step and his efforts are highly praised.

As children develop out of the scribble stage, they learn to control the direction of a line. Up and down and sideways the child begins to consciously arrange his lines on the paper.

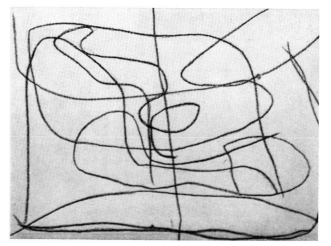

He learns that he can turn and bend them at will. Now his lines begin to show some degree of conscious control and planning. The edges of his paper become a frame within which to work. Some of his lines go up and down and side to side to repeat the verticals and horizontals of the paper.

He discovers that he can turn a line back on itself to make a circular shape. Now he fills his paper with these new curved forms, often joining one loop to another in an endless chain.

But don't expect consistent progress each day. A sheet filled with carefully drawn lines and circular shapes suddenly may be completely covered with seemingly vicious scribbles. And don't be surprised when a beautiful drawing is crumpled and thrown in the wastebasket. Remember, the child is not producing something

The young child learns he can turn and bend his lines into circular forms, often joining one loop to another in an endless chain.

Often a child's first recognizable symbol is a human figure. No body; just head, arms and legs. He is drawing what is important to him and what he understands.

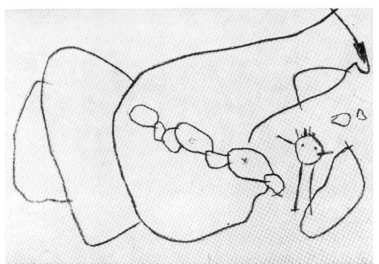

As he grows in awareness and understanding of the human figure, he adds the body and such details as fingers and hair to his drawings.

for us but for himself. He will not always wish to share it.

Often a child's first recognizable symbol is a human figure. One of his circular shapes will be given eyes, two lines to represent arms and another pair of lines to suggest legs. No body; just head, arms and legs. It may be Daddy or Mother or "me." With only slight variations the symbol becomes a dog, a cow or a horse.

These first symbols are a giant step forward and should be received with much praise and encouragement. But at this point the adult must keep in mind that *the child is drawing not what he sees but what he knows and understands.* Only those aspects of the objects which are meaningful to him are included. For example, in representing a person the head is important because it contains the eyes for seeing, a nose

Children soon like to draw themselves in various situations such as eating, skating or grumpily brushing teeth.

for smelling and a mouth for eating and talking. At first the ears may not be included since he is not so conscious of the act of hearing. But the youngster who is constantly urged to comb his hair or the girl whose mother spends considerable time in brushing and arranging curls may include this aspect of the figure in exaggerated form.

At first the body itself is of small consequence and is usually omitted in the drawing. Later it may make a first appearance in a much smaller form than the head. Remember, the size of objects in children's drawings is determined by their relative importance *to the child*.

As children develop interest in drawing people and objects around them, they may be encouraged to draw themselves involved in various activities such as combing their hair, eating candy or skating. Our objective is not to teach the young child how *we* think he should draw, but to encourage him to express *his own ideas* in his drawings *in his own way*. His way is not our way nor the way of other boys and girls in the classroom.

Young children are encouraged to draw on the chalk-board. We never compare or point out that one is better or more "real" than another because this discourages originality and creative thinking.

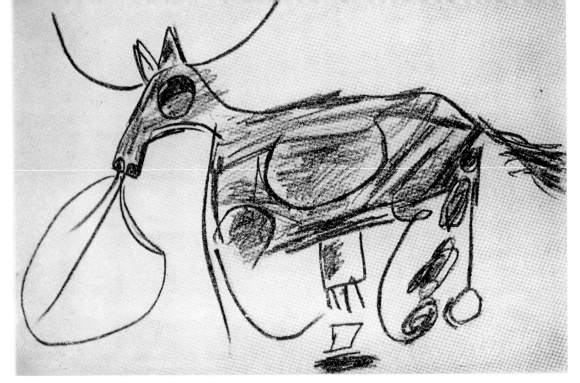

Children are encouraged to draw things in their own way as they see and understand them. What makes a cow look like a cow? Horns, milk bag and faucets, of course.

Drawing is a completely personal activity and to have successful drawing activities we must respect and completely enjoy the child's original and unique method of expression. Remember that there is no one "correct" way of drawing anything. The finest compliment we can make about each child's work is to recognize its uniqueness.

"What a fine drawing you have made, John. I like it because you have drawn it in your own way. It isn't like any other drawing in the room."

The moment we begin to compare drawings by children, pointing out that one is better or more "real" than another, we are discouraging the very originality and creative thinking we seek.

Drawing is a basic activity in the kindergarten. For most children it is a natural, happy activity. We laugh *with* children about their drawings, and never *at* them. We genuinely like children's drawings and let them know that we enjoy their work.

Remember, the *good* drawing is one in which the child puts something of himself. It is an honest original idea of his own.

Painting

MATERIALS:
jars of water-base paint
bristle brushes
18" x 24" paper
newspapers
sponges for cleanup

Painting is a completely new experience for most kindergartners. At home, many have had access to pencils and crayons, but relatively few have worked with brush and paints.

In many ways this fact plays to our advantage. Children have few if any preconceived notions of what their paintings should look like. They are excited about the new experience and look forward to their first paintings with great eagerness. There is a much greater chance for complete honesty of personal expression in paintings than drawings because some parents try to push children in drawing, even drawing things for them to copy. Too, there is a tendency to grip the crayon or pencil so tightly that the work is cramped and small. The long handled brush with its wide set of bristles suggests a bigger, freer approach.

Equipment

Most kindergarten rooms are equipped with several double easels. The paint trays hold jars of fresh paint at all times so that children during free time can paint if they choose to do so.

However, these easels provide painting facilities for relatively few children. A better solution is a small table or tote–cart on wheels to serve as our main source of painting equipment. Here we keep a larger number of jars of paint, each with its own brush, a supply of 18" x 24" newsprint paper, a stack of old newspapers to spread on tables or floors and moist sponges for cleanup. Most of the painting will be done on the floor, the furniture moved to one side if possible. Or the children may squat or sit in aisles between desks or tables and around the edge of the room.

Most kindergarten teachers use powder paints because they are cheaper than premixed

Small-sized easels are desirable but provide painting area for relatively few children. Most painting is done on the floor between tables and around edges of the room.

Photo: Rochester, N. Y., Public Schools

tempera or poster paints. There are few advantages to the premixed paint, and if there is a question of budget it is better to have a larger quantity of powder paint and a wider variety of colors. In a school year a class of 24 children can easily use up a dozen one pound cans each of red, yellow, green, blue, purple, orange, brown, black and white. Of course, the amount of paint used will be determined primarily by the amount of time and emphasis placed upon painting activities.

School supply catalogs list easel brushes. These brushes have long handles and the best quality have seamless metal ferrules. Brushes with stiff bristles approximately 1″ long are preferable. The bristles are set in glue so we avoid washing them in *hot* water which tends to dissolve the glue. A supply of approximately 36 brushes might include 18 brushes ¼″ wide and 18 brushes ½″ wide.

Unprinted newsprint 18″ x 24″ in size may be purchased by the ream (500 sheets). A ream provides 24 youngsters with about 20 paintings each, but the paper will be used in so many different ways in the classroom that the purchase of 5 or 6 reams for the year is recommended. If half-sized sheets (12″ x 18″) are needed for other activities, it is easy to cut the large sheets in half on a large paper cutter.

Mixing Paints

We can't avoid an occasional spilled jar of paint, so jars are kept not more than one-third full. To prepare the paint, place four to six tablespoons of dry powder paint in a pint jar, add just enough water to make a paste, then add additional water to make the paint creamy in consistency. Avoid watery paint; it is difficult to control and lacks brilliance. Paint should be thin enough to flow easily and thick enough so one can not see the paper through it.

Because evaporation causes the paint to thicken, teachers should keep jars tightly capped between painting sessions, especially over week ends. Much time can be saved if all jars and caps are the same size. For this purpose, wide-mouth peanut butter jars are ideal. They hold a pint, and their low, big shape does not easily tip.

As in drawing, first paintings by very young children are meaningless blobs of color. As a first step, they should be praised and the child encouraged to fill his space with rich, beautiful color.

Photo: Maplewood, Missouri, Public Schools

24

Smocks

Some type of smock should be required for painting activities. This may vary from one of dad's old shirts with sleeves cut short to a rectangle of oil cloth with a hole in the middle to slip over the head.

Beginning Painting

Large sheets of 18″ x 24″ newsprint are fine for painting. Children are encouraged to work big, filling space from top to bottom and side to side.

Photo: Chicago Public Schools

There is no one accepted method of presenting painting to young children. Some teachers set out several relatively deep colors such as red, blue, green and purple. Each child is invited to choose one color. This dark color makes a strong and satisfying contrast against the light paper. Yellow and orange are not included in these first paintings since their contrast with the paper is rather weak. After several painting experiences, the child is encouraged to choose two colors, perhaps one light and one dark, and then three and four colors.

Other teachers like to introduce painting experiences by "painting" on the chalkboard with water. The child knows that his picture will soon dry away and he is free to paint as large as he likes. Meanwhile he is learning always to put on his smock for painting and something about the care of brushes, to set his jar where it won't be easily tipped over and other necessary disciplines.

Of course there are disciplines—or restrictions—in art activities just as there are in other school activities. For example, children should learn to take care of brushes and to drag a loaded brush across the *inside* of the jar to remove surplus paint which otherwise may drip on the floor, table or down a painting. He should learn to pick up his papers from the floor, where to take his painting to dry, to wash up spots of paint from the floor or table with a moist sponge and to hang up his smock before returning to his seat.

It is a kindness to the child to teach him responsibility. And responsibility includes his obligation to help clean up the room after art activities. A period of time for cleanup should be planned as a basic part of the activity period.

Soon the children will take this for granted and, if held to relatively high standards, will take pride in seeing that the room is left in good order. Large sponges, kept where they are accessible to the children, are basic items for painting activities.

What to Paint

Some five-year-olds are still in the scribble stage. Their first paintings will be limited to masses of one or more colors which show little conscious control. As in the case of drawing, these should be complimented and the child should feel secure that his teacher likes and approves of what he is doing. It is especially important that he be praised for his efforts if others around him are more mature in their painting. If he is made to feel that his paintings are not acceptable he will avoid painting activities and there will be an unnatural delay in his development.

We do not criticize the *way* a child paints an object. The importance of his expression lies primarily in his ability to express his own personal reactions and feelings. We are interested in the personal interpretation he makes of the world as he understands it. This interpretation should not reflect that of his teacher, parents or classmates.

We do make efforts to enlarge the understanding of the child's world. And as the child grows in his understanding, knowledge and awareness of things, this will be reflected in his paintings. For example, take the painting of trees. We would never, under any circumstances, tell a four- or five-year-old how we think he should paint a tree. This would be requiring him to express *our* understanding of a tree rather than *his*. However, without ever referring to drawing or painting, we look at trees together and discuss them: how they grow, the bigness of the trunk, how the branches spread out, how leaves group themselves around the branches. We are learning; we are becoming *aware*. And as we become *aware* of things, we include this *awareness* in our paintings—gradually and slowly. And much more slowly for some than for others. Our job is to provide opportunities for this type of growth and development.

Children enjoy coming to the front of the room, holding up their paintings and telling

Kindergartners enjoy group painting on long sheets of wrapping paper. Each fills in his designated area and shares in the pleasure of the completed "mural."

other children about them. If the painting is still in the scribble stage, it may be referred to as a *design* and the child can name and point out the different colors he has used. When children reach the stage of including symbols of reality in their paintings, usually they are anxious to talk and tell stories about them. This verbalizing about their work is entirely healthy and should be encouraged. Far from being disturbed by the element of fantasy in his art and story telling, encourage this use of the imagination. If a cow can jump over the moon in children's literature, nothing is impossible in his own creative imagination. So explore and exploit the child's interest in fantasy. It will do more to develop his creativity than a hundred dull facts.

Displaying Paintings

Paintings should be put up on the walls for everyone to enjoy. Each child should be represented regardless of the stage of his development. In case wall space does not permit large paintings by each child at one time, this should be explained to the children so they will know that each will have his work displayed over a period of time.

Murals

Although most paintings will be done on individual sheets of paper, young children enjoy a group painting activity in which everyone works together on a large sheet of wrapping paper. Each may be assigned an area to fill in as he wishes and the big mural may be put up on the bulletin board or out in the corridor for all to see and enjoy. Such a project provides many opportunities for learning to share and work cooperatively.

The Importance of Painting

It has been my experience that more kindergarten children enjoy painting experiences and derive more personal satisfaction from them than perhaps any other type of art activity. Young children seem to be natural painters. The directness and complete honesty of their expressions and total lack of fear are the envy of professional artists. Certainly the charm, the freshness and spontaneity of their work have great appeal to all who delight in child art.

We do not criticize the way a child paints. We are interested in the personal interpretation he makes of the world as he understands it. This interpretation should not reflect that of his teacher, parents or classmates.

Photo: Seattle, Washington, Public Schools

Clay

MATERIALS:
water-base clay
12" x 15" board
newspapers

"Ooh! It's cool and soft like mud. I like to make mud pies. See, I'm going to make lots of mud pies. Then I'm going to play like I eat them all up."

"Listen! My clay makes funny noises. When I squeeze it through my hands it goes sqush, squnch, squlsh!"

These boys and girls are having their first experience with clay. It is a water-base type sometimes called firing or pottery clay. It is different from oil-base, non-hardening clays such as Plasticene because it will dry when exposed to the air. It is much easier to manipulate than Plasticene and, let's face it, somewhat messier. But who ever said we had to stay neat and clean all the time? We teach children how to protect tables and desks with newspapers and to wipe up stray bits of clay from the floor with a damp sponge.

Young children are encouraged to experiment to find out what clay will do. They push,

punch and pull it into many forms and shapes. When a child has reached the stage of making objects, he is encouraged to try people and animals. He is praised for his efforts no matter how simple his symbols may be.

In modeling an animal or a person the young child learns that heavy bodies cannot be supported by long, slender legs. So that they won't break easily, objects modeled in clay must be thick with no small parts extending from the central form.

By pressing his thumb into a ball of clay and pushing outwards, the kindergartner can make his first piece of pottery—a pinch pot. He should be shown how to smooth the walls of clay with his fingers to avoid cracks in the edges that weaken the structure.

Depending on the thickness of clay objects, they may take a week or two to dry. They should be dried slowly and evenly in a place free from cold or hot drafts of air. They may

A thin board about 12" x 15" is fine to work on. The reverse side of oil cloth also makes a good surface because clay doesn't stick to it. Encouraged to experiment to find out what clay will do, young children push, pound and pull it into many different shapes.

Photo: Play Schools Association, New York City

Orange sticks and other simple wooden tools supplement finger manipulation as children develop in their understanding of clay as an art medium.

Photo: New York City Public Schools

be left in their natural clay color or painted with powder paint.

Clay may be purchased in dry or moist form in amounts from 50 to 500 pounds. The new plastic sacks make it possible to add a bit of water to the dry clay flour and knead it to the right consistency without removing it from the sack. But it is simpler to buy it already mixed if the budget permits.

It is not difficult to organize the room for clay work. There should be an airtight container to hold the clay. This may be a heavy

From a round ball of clay, the child develops a pinch pot by first pressing his thumbs into the clay and gradually pushing outward. He learns to smooth the walls to avoid cracks.

In making animals and figures, children learn to exaggerate the size of legs in order to support a heavy body. Each part must be firmly attached and smoothed to avoid cracking in drying.

crock or a garbage can with a tight-fitting lid. Children should be taught always to replace the lid in order to keep the clay moist and pliable. This means soft enough to manipulate easily but not so soft that it is sticky.

A stock of old newspapers near the container of clay helps the children learn to protect desks and tables. A few thin 12″ x 15″ boards are fine to work on but are not required. A ball of clay somewhat smaller than a baseball is sufficient for each child during an activity period. Of course, all the children needn't work with clay at one time. Six or eight youngsters may choose clay while others work with less messy materials.

Although not necessary, a second container may be kept available to hold used clay that has dried out. Wrapped in a damp cloth, such as an old bath towel, this clay will absorb enough moisture to be used again.

It is important that three-dimensional materials such as clay be included in the art program and that they be made available frequently during the year. Sometimes a child who shows little interest in drawing and painting may find considerable satisfaction in working with clay.

Weaving

MATERIALS:
5 feet of ¾" x 1⅜" wood
12—1½" nails with heads
1 small box 1" finishing nails
sandpaper, ruler and pencil
hammer and saw
twine and heavy rug yarns

A simple loom is a fascinating plaything for a four-year-old, and five-year-olds will be eager to produce a finished product. Here is a good solution for Mother's Day or Christmas gifts. Best of all, the loom is inexpensive, easy to make and operate.

Too often, weaving at this age level is limited to the manipulation of paper or felt strips. Many young children find paper weaving difficult to do and others do not derive much personal satisfaction either from the activity or the resulting product. The simple loom illustrated here interests young children and yet is not beyond their manipulative ability.

For four-year-olds, warp strings are placed 1" apart so that it is not hard for young fingers to manipulate the yarn. No one is disturbed if a mistake is made and we are not concerned whether an object is completed.

Constructing the loom is simple. We recommend ¾" x 1⅜" pine. Ask your lumber yard for "blind stop." It sells for about 8 cents per running foot. The two short strips across the top are 12" long, the two longer side strips 14" long. After the strips are well sanded, four nails are used at *each* corner joint to make the frame rigid.

Next a pencil line is drawn down the center of the two short strips and a ruler is used to measure dots at ½" intervals. These penciled dots serve as a guide for driving 1" finishing nails halfway into the wood. Slant them a bit outward from the center of the loom so the warp threads will not slip off.

The loom is now ready to be "warped" (threaded for weaving). For first experiences in weaving, the warp thread should be heavy twine tied to a corner nail and then wound back and forth around the nails from one end of the loom to the other. A space of 1" between threads is desirable at first. In this case the twine must pass around three nails at each end of the loom.

For weaving, heavy cotton rug yarn ¼" thick is suggested. If you can not purchase this heavy weight yarn locally, you will find it listed in Sears, Roebuck catalog. Buy several colors including black and white. Cut it into strips 16" long which will permit each piece to extend about 2" on each side of the loom.

Now we are ready to weave. Gather a group of children around for a demonstration. Choose two colors of yarn, perhaps one light and one dark color. Using a length of yarn, show how the fingers lead the yarn through the warp threads—over one and under one, over one and under one. When the length of yarn has been threaded across the loom, push it down to one end of the loom until it touches the nails. Be sure that an equal amount of yarn extends beyond the loom on each side.

The secret of weaving, we explain, is that each time we start across the warp threads with a new piece of yarn, we go *over* the thread we went *under* before, and *under* the thread we went *over* before. When we have taken the

Having experimented with the 1" loom, a five-year-old graduates to the ½" loom which is more challenging. Using lengths of heavy rug yarn she learns to alternate colors with seldom a mistake in colors or weaving.

The weaving is completed and it is time to remove the woven mat from the loom. The slanted nail heads have prevented the taut warp strings from slipping off during the weaving process. Now the weaving is carefully lifted off the loom.

second piece of yarn clear across the warp, we use our fingers to push it up close to the first row and again make sure that an equal amount of yarn extends beyond the loom on each side. Now we are ready for the third row. It is as easy as that!

To do successful weaving, we must think and watch closely what we are doing. We can not chatter and talk while we weave. But we do not get upset when a mistake is made. Weaving is a *game* at first with no thought of finishing an article.

When a child has mastered the basic technique of weaving, we can warp the loom with half-inch spaces. This is done by winding the twine around *two* nails at each end of the loom instead of *three*. It will require greater dexterity to weave the yarn over and under this warp, but most five-year-olds will be eager to complete the weaving of a simple mat. When the loom is filled with weaving (be sure the weaving fills the space right up to the nails) it is lifted off the loom. If a sewing machine is handy, mother or teacher may sew along the sides to "lock" the yarn in place. Now the loom is ready to be warped again with string for another weaving experience.

A problem in getting looms made for the kindergarten room? Ask a group of fifth or sixth grade boys to take over the project of making six or eight looms for the kindergarten room. They will do a fine job. But better have some extra wood at hand. They will probably want to make a loom for themselves, placing the finishing nails closer together for more complex weaving projects.

The mat's open sides pose a problem which requires the help of an adult and a sewing machine. Sewing along both sides of the mat locks the loose ends of the yarn.

Building with Blocks

MATERIALS:
commercially made blocks
or scraps of wood

Wooden blocks delight young children. They like to hold them, push them, lift them and carry them around. Their special design makes these blocks easy to arrange and rearrrange in constructions that provide many kinds of learning experiences. Through experimentation, the child learns principles of balance and he gets the satisfaction of achieving orderly arrangements.

A father handy with a saw can make a fine set of building blocks, but an assortment of wood scraps collected from a building site will also do nicely.

You can buy a number of different types of blocks. Large hollow blocks may be bought singly or in sets. These are brick-like shapes of varying sizes that young children can handle easily. The kindergarten room should also have some of the solid unit blocks in brick shapes, wedges, arches and cylinders.

For individual block building we choose a space at least six feet square outside lanes of class traffic. The blocks should be stacked near this working space and arranged so that children may choose from a variety of shapes and sizes as they build. Children should be taught to put the blocks away in an orderly fashion.

At first a young child may prefer working alone while he gets used to the shapes of blocks, tests their weight and learns how to handle them.

At first it is usually best for a child to work alone with the blocks. With no interference from other children he tests their shapes, weight and strength.

The wise teacher avoids making too many suggestions during these early explorations. Gradually the child gains confidence in his ability to handle the blocks. He learns to stack them successfully, to build and construct with balance and stability. We do not insist on an explanation of what he has built. But we find occasion to compliment each child upon his ideas and express pleasure when he achieves a sturdy construction.

Don't be surprised if a delicately balanced construction is suddenly knocked down. This is a harmless expression of pent-up feelings. In fact, occasionally we may envy the child's opportunity to completely smash what he has built.

After a child has had opportunity to work independently he is usually eager for cooperative building projects that involve two or more children. This of course requires a larger space and more blocks. Working together children learn to exchange ideas, to discuss possible solutions to a problem and to help each other toward common goals.

Having gained some confidence in using blocks, he will welcome an admiring observer.

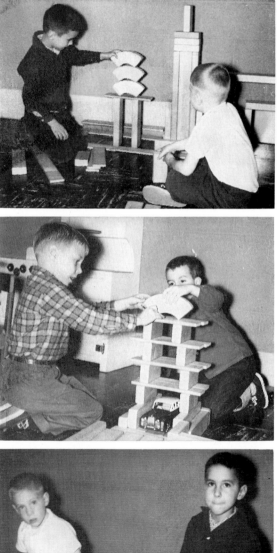

Soon he will enjoy sharing a construction project with a friend.

Teamwork in building is followed by cooperative helping in cleaning up and putting blocks away for another day.

Puppets

MATERIALS:
small paper sacks
Dad's old sock
worn-out light bulbs
paint
scrap materials

For children with a flair for dramatics, hand puppets do great things. For the timid child who feels insecure and self-conscious in front of others, what better stimulation than to allow him to make a puppet and bring it to life with words he chooses and speaks?

Kings and queens, firemen and police, "good" children and "bad" ones take on a new enchantment as hand puppets. They provide endless opportunities for dramatic play and make it possible for children to talk and express ideas without embarrassment or self consciousness.

His first hand puppet may well represent the child himself. It can describe personal experiences that the child hesitates to tell the group. Shy Sandra, for example, lets her puppet tell about a trip to the country or how she helped Mother clean up her room.

Children can plan short plays to present before the group or for parents visiting the classroom. Roles are never memorized but are spoken naturally and freely. How much more meaningful it becomes when children let their puppets talk about good manners and eating habits! A puppet's accident in crossing a street without looking first for cars becomes an exciting, not-soon-forgotten lesson in safety.

Children often reveal some new facet of their personalities when given the opportunity to

A simple hand puppet can be made by pasting crayon drawing on a paper sack filled with shredded newspaper. A stick is inserted in the sack for the child to hold.

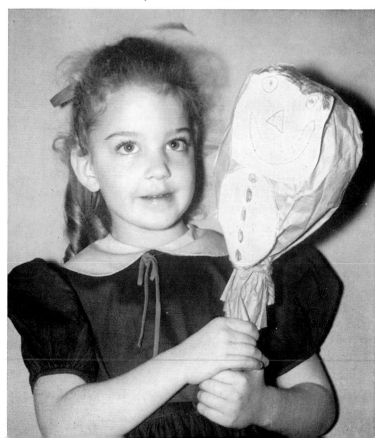

A sock puppet is made by filling the toe of one of Dad's old socks with rags, pushing a stick up into the rags and tying a bit of cloth around the neck. Tempera paint is used to make the features plus yarn for hair.

play with puppets during free time. These informal and unrehearsed experiences in dramatic play help alert parents and teachers to learn more about their children.

Can kindergartners make their own puppets? Yes, there are several easy methods. Perhaps the simplest of all is for the child to color or paint a figure on a sheet of paper, cut it out and paste it on a flat stick. Some of the children will make birds and butterflies and help them "fly" around the room. Animals are always popular, but *people* are favored subjects because *they* can talk.

A paper sack puppet is easy to make. The sack may be as small as a candy sack or as big as a grocery sack. It is filled with torn strips of paper and a stick is inserted so that it extends almost to the top. Then teacher helps tie a string tightly around the "neck." The face may be drawn or painted on a separate sheet of paper, cut out and pasted on the front of the sack or it may be painted directly on the sack before it is filled.

Old light bulbs make fine puppet heads. A scrap of fabric tied around the base suggests clothes. Tempera paint is used to paint the features of the face, and yarn or bits of raveled rope are glued on for hair. (Fast drying airplane cement is most satisfactory for this.)

Then there is always the sock puppet made by filling the toe of one of Dad's old socks with rags, pushing a thin stick up into the rags and tying a bit of cloth around the neck. Again, tempera paint works fine for the features and yarn or string for hair can be glued or tacked on with thread. At home a table, or at school teacher's desk makes an acceptable stage. Children crouch behind it, holding their puppets so that they show just above the top surface.

Brown wrapping paper scotch-taped across the front of a card table creates an open stage, or a large cardboard carton can be cut out and painted to make a more elaborate theater.

Children are easily satisfied with the simplest equipment. The opportunity to act and speak is the big excitement, so don't worry about details. Whether it is a rainy day at home or a special day at school, on with the show!

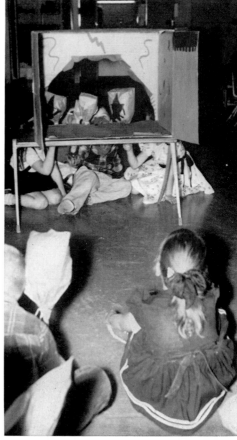

A large cardboard carton can be cut out and painted to make an effective puppet stage.

A scrap of cloth is tied around the base of an old light bulb, and tempera paint is used to paint the features.

Stitchery

MATERIALS:
onion sacks
plastic screen wire
tapestry needles
heavy yarns

Are kindergartners too young to do stitchery? Not if we accept their limitations and use appropriate materials. Young children are interested in learning how to use a needle and are eager to experiment with sewing techniques. However, it should be understood that we merely *introduce* stitchery at this level and hold our standards within easy reach of the average child.

Wide-meshed materials are used as a structural base for designs in colored yarns. A potato or onion sack works fine and children can ask parents to save them for classroom use. Place a piece of cardboard inside the sack, as near the size of the sack as possible. This makes it easier for the child to hold and keeps his stitches from going through both thicknesses of the bag. Use a large dull-pointed tapestry needle and heavy cotton or wool yarns.

Encourage the children to choose two or perhaps three colors to work with. They can fill their needles with these colors several times as they work to fill the space. Some of the children will have difficulty in threading the yarn through the eye of the needle, but many will catch on quickly and help the others. Show how the end of the yarn can be tied to the loosely woven material and then how the needle can go over and under a thread of the mesh to make beautiful lines of color. Encourage them to go all the way across the bag instead of working in just one corner.

A wide-meshed potato or onion sack is a good structural base for beginning stitchery. A piece of cardboard is placed inside the sack to make it easier to handle. Dull-pointed tapestry needles and heavy cotton or wool yarns are used for stitchery.

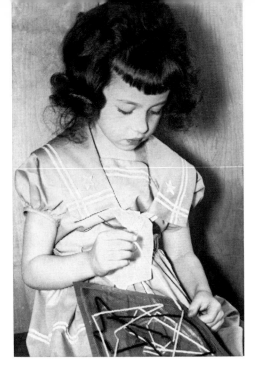

Plastic screen wire edged with adhesive tape makes a fine base for Sandra's stitchery design.

Hot pads are made from four squares of fabric. Using a large darning needle threaded with heavy cotton or lightweight wool, a simple over-stitch ½″ deep is used to bind the edges.

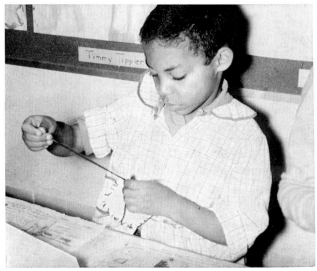

Explain that it isn't necessary to go over and under every thread. It is quite all right to jump over a few threads at one time. However, we must not get in a hurry. If the yarn jumps too fast the entire design will be too loose. If we pull the threads too tightly our stitchery won't stay flat and even.

When the stitchery is completed the sack may be cut so that just the top side which contains the design may be mounted on a sheet of construction paper. The stapling machine is fine for doing this. Now, how about a display on a corridor bulletin board?

Another good base for stitchery is plastic screen wire. (Metal screen wire is too prickly, hard to cut and will not give sufficiently to permit large-eyed needles to pass through the holes.) The edges may be bound with adhesive tape. Use the same tapestry needle and yarn recommended for onion sack stitchery.

If your children enjoyed this project, how about some more needle work? Hot pads make fine gifts for Christmas. Using a 6″ square of cardboard as a guide, children can place it on a piece of fabric and cut out four squares. These are then pinned together. Using a large darning needle threaded with heavy cotton or lightweight yarn, a simple over-stitch about ½″ deep is used to bind the edges. If a solid light colored fabric has been chosen, children can decorate the pad with designs in crayons. They will be delighted with the results and Mother has a new hot pad for handling those kitchen utensils.

Finger Painting

MATERIALS:
finger paint
(commercial or make your own)
glazed paper

Finger painting provides opportunities for big rhythmic movements of the hands and arms and, according to some educators, tends to have a calming effect on youngsters when they are keyed up and tense.

In a sense finger painting is poorly named because it should not be limited to just drawing with a finger. This often seems to be the extent of the activity. Adults should experiment with finger paint themselves before introducing it to children so they will understand its possibilities.

Finger paint is a slippery, water-base paint which can be purchased from almost any firm that handles school paints. It can also be made by parent or teacher. There are a number of basic recipes, but an effective one costing about 20 cents can be made right in the kitchen or classroom. It uses these ingredients:

One 12 oz. box of Faultless starch (or other cold water starch)

An equal quantity of soap flakes (such as Ivory or Lux)

Two cups of cold water

Powder paint for coloring

Mix together the starch and soap flakes. Slowly add the water while stirring. Mix and beat until it reaches the consistency of whipped potatoes. Add powder or tempera paint to get the desired color, keeping in mind that dark colors show up more effectively than light colors in final paintings. The recipe will make about one and a half pints, sufficient for an average size class.

Debbie smoothes the finger paint across the paper with the palms of both hands. By pressing hard she begins to create a design of zig-zag movements.

She learns to double up her fist and make big circular designs. Teacher's demonstration shows her how to use the side of hand, knuckles, several fingers or thumb— seldom just one finger alone.

Finger painting is done on a glazed paper that has been well moistened so that the paint slides easily over the surface. An absorbent paper such as newsprint or manila is unsatisfactory. Regular finger painting paper may be purchased, or glazed shelf paper from the five-and-ten or butcher paper which can be purchased in rolls are usable.

Other necessary equipment includes a bucket of water for washing hands, if there is no sink in the room, a sponge or two and smocks for the youngsters.

The paper may be dipped in a container of water, or the dry paper can be put in place and a wet sponge run over it several times. If there is a Formica-covered counter in your kitchen, this is an ideal place for finger painting in the home. At school, if tables or desks have good coats of varnish there is no danger of hurting them since a wet sponge will quickly remove all traces of the finger paint at the conclusion of the activity.

For a first experience in finger painting, give just enough of a demonstration to convince the children that the activity is fun and that they need have no fear of getting their hands in the paint. After wetting the paper and placing a spoonful of paint in the middle, place both hands flat on the paint and begin to spread it evenly over the surface. Here you may exclaim how cool and smooth it feels—to set aside the child's fear of getting his hands dirty. (Remember how often children are admonished to keep themselves *clean*. No wonder when merely *told* to put their hands in finger paint they often place their hands behind their backs and say, "I don't want to. It's dirty!")

Once the paint has been smoothed across the paper to an even consistency, explain that it takes pressure to push *through* the paint and show the white paper beneath to make a design. Emphasize big hand movements rather than finger drawing. Double up the fist to make big, sweeping circles across the surface. Then

Karen paints a picture of herself in the woods, uses forefinger for outline. Later she adds bushes at the base using side of hand in strokes that push upward from bottom of the paper.

show how with the palm of the hand the paint may be smoothed out and made ready for another design.

Show how the side of the hand, the knuckles, several fingers together or the thumb can make different shapes. Don't try to make any recognizable shapes, for this may frustrate the child, convincing him that he can't do as well as you. The only purpose in the demonstration is to make the child *want* to experiment and look forward to the activity himself. Refer to the paintings, if you like, as *designs*. There need be no other meaning until and unless the child begins, of his own accord, to make recognizable shapes.

If the paint dries out squeeze a few drops of water from the sponge directly on to the paper. The paint may now be smoothed out again.

When a painting is made that satisfies the child so that he wants to keep it, put the paper aside to dry—perhaps on newspapers at the edge of the room. Or, better still, it may be draped over a portable wooden clothes dryer. This is an excellent space-saver for drying all kinds of paintings and can be folded up and stored when necessary.

When finger paintings are entirely dry they often are so badly curled and warped that they are difficult to display in the room. This problem is easily corrected by pressing them flat with a warm iron.

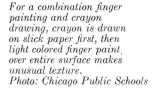

For a combination finger painting and crayon drawing, crayon is drawn on slick paper first, then light colored finger paint over entire surface makes unusual texture.
Photo: Chicago Public Schools

Cut Paper

MATERIALS:
12″ x 16″ colored construction papers
blunt-nosed scissors
library paste

Blunt-nosed scissors, a dab of paste on a piece of paper and some bright colored construction papers provide many opportunities for creative expression. No pencils allowed—we cut directly from the colored papers without any preliminary drawing.

Cutting and tearing bright colored paper, arranging the pieces and pasting them down are processes particularly well suited to the kindergarten level. Colored 9″ x 12″ construction paper is adequate for some activities, but larger sheets are needed so often that it is just as well to invest in 12″ x 18″ stock. Teachers find it is helpful to have on hand one or two packages of 18″ x 24″ paper in assorted colors to use as backgrounds on the bulletin board or to back a child's drawing or painting when it is displayed.

Blunt-nosed scissors and a dab of paste on a piece of paper are all the children need besides the colored papers. (Some parents and teachers working with smaller groups will prefer scissors with medium points.) If sheets of colored papers are spread out on a table at the front of the room, children can choose the colors they want to work with at their own tables. A shirt or suit box can hold the larger scraps, and children should be encouraged to use paper from this box whenever possible.

Preliminary drawing is not advisable because children tend to draw small details that will not lend themselves to cutting or tearing. This is especially true if children are allowed to use pencils. So let's make it a rule that we never use pencils in art activities at the kindergarten level.

To tear out shapes, children need to learn how to control the torn edge by moving their fingers inch by inch as they tear. They must realize they can't control the direction of a long tear. In practice, many young children find tearing paper rather difficult. Most children prefer to cut their paper since they have better control of the process.

A 12″ x 18″ sheet provides a good background for most designs or pictures. Larger sheets are suitable for more elaborate projects when several children work together.

At the upper grade levels the students generally cut out all the shapes first and then plan an arrangement of them on the background paper. Kindergartners often prefer to cut and paste each shape as it is produced. As in

First we work on individual pictures, filling the space with ideas so that there are no lonely looking spots.

painting, the teacher may use questions to encourage a consideration of color choices, darks and lights.

"How many have chosen a background paper that is light in color? Will light or dark colors show up best against your paper? Name some colors you might use."

Again as in painting, space-filling problems are considered. Children are often satisfied to paste an animal, house or person in the middle of the paper and then consider their work finished. The parent and teacher should stimulate and encourage the child to add interest to his work through the addition of related ideas.

This type of directed teaching should not inhibit or discourage children if used in moderation. In fact, the final work is more satisfying to the child because he has done more creative thinking about it.

"Mary, do you have an idea for your paper picture today?"

"Yes, I'm going to show Twinkie, my cat."

"A fine idea. What will your cat be doing?"

"He's drinking milk out of his bowl."

"Where is the bowl?"

"On the kitchen floor beside the stove."

"Then what else besides Twinkie can you put in your picture to make it interesting?"

"Well, I can show Twinkie, his bowl, and the stove and the kitchen table and maybe a chair . . ."

"And maybe you?"

"Yes, me pouring the milk."

"Those are all wonderful ideas. Mary is sure to have a beautiful picture today because she has thought of many different things to put in her picture."

Children readily see they can add small decorative elements to large areas such as slender strips of paper for stripes and bits of squares or circles for polka dots. These additions will enrich the design and add interest to the total composition.

Later we plan cooperative group projects which will fill the bulletin board. Each child selects the parts he wishes to make and completes them at his work table.

What standards, if any, do we set up regarding neatness in cutting and pasting activities? Some children have little difficulty in learning how to paste. Others apparently can't open the jar of paste without getting it all over them as well as their work.

There is no question that originality in developing ideas tops our list in evaluating art activities at the kindergarten level just as at upper grade levels. On the other hand, having ideas is not the whole story in art, or in life. We must develop skills necessary to carry out our ideas effectively. Therefore, teachers need not fear mentioning neatness in art work so long as they make it clear that neatness is only *one* characteristic in effective art expression. Everyone has seen displays of kindergarten art products that are neat, identical and sterile. We much prefer messy Marty who is full of interesting and original ideas to prim Pete who is neat but never has an idea of his own. It is Marty who one day may make an important contribution to society because of his ability to think creatively. Keep him busy with praise and encouragement. Gradually help him to become aware of the importance of carrying out his work carefully. Remember, however, that nagging is apt to convince him that art activities are not for him.

Together the children decide where the parts will go on the bulletin board, overlapping some shapes to make them friendly with each other.

Box Animals

MATERIALS:
small boxes
airplane cement
paints

Milk cartons, cosmetic boxes, stationary boxes, hose boxes, boxes for toothpaste, adhesive tape, pencils, ink—the children will search at home and school for all kinds of small and medium sized cardboard boxes in preparation for the day we make box animals. We pile them up in a corner of the room or put them all in a large grocery carton.

But before we ask the children to find all these boxes, they should have some idea of *why* they are looking for them. Teachers sometimes complain that children do not remember to bring items from home. A note to Mother helps, but first the children should know what the activity is all about. When Mother logically asks, "What are you going to do with a bunch of old boxes?", children should never have to answer, "I don't know. The teacher just said to bring them."

So our first responsibility is to present the activity in such a way that the children are stimulated into action. It is *not* recommended that the teacher bring to class a box animal that she has made in a college class. The adult-made animal will have a professional look to the child which may evoke admiration but actually may be discouraging in terms of his own abilities.

It will be much better just to bring to class a number of boxes which she has found. Why not dramatize the situation a bit to increase the curiosity and interest of the children? For example, when the children first come into the room they might see a large grocery sack tightly closed on the teacher's desk. What is in it? There is a short guessing game with the teacher joining in the fun. Finally she opens the sack and pours out all the little boxes she has collected. Yes, they are empty. But they can be made into many strange and wonderful things. What are some of the things we can make with them, she asks. Playfully she stacks one on the other. What does it suggest to the children? Who will help her choose a box which might be the body of an imaginary animal? Is there a box which could represent

What can you make with a group of small boxes? A bird? A person? An animal? Which box would make a good body? A neck? A head?

Rickie attaches the boxes together with a fast-drying airplane cement. In a few minutes they will be ready to paint.

a neck? A head? A tail? What about legs? Of course, our animal doesn't *have* to have legs and it may be difficult to find four boxes suitable for them.

How can we make the boxes stay together? A good solution is a tube of fast-drying airplane cement purchased from a hobby shop. Ordinary paste or glue is not suitable for this purpose. There are also paper fasteners and in some cases a stapling machine comes in handy. But the fast-drying cement is best. So with the help of a couple of youngsters you glue the parts together and set them aside to dry. The children can think up a name for the animal, decide where it lives and even make up stories about adventures it might have.

There are several important factors to remember about this type of presentation. First, the teacher has not produced anything in order to show how clever she is. She has planned carefully so that the children have participated *with her* in using the materials *from the beginning*. They have been personally involved in discovering what might be made with the boxes. They are personally excited about how the boxes can be joined together to represent an animal—based either upon a real or imaginary animal. They have participated in exploring the possibilities of making the boxes stay together as a unit with glue, paper fasteners or staples. They have used their imaginations in thinking up an appropriate name for

A bit of detergent added to tempera or powder paint will make it stick to the glazed surface of boxes. For choices of color we let our imagination run free.

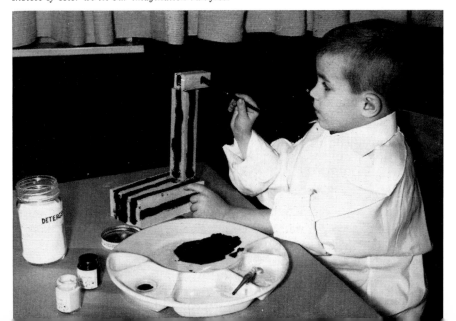

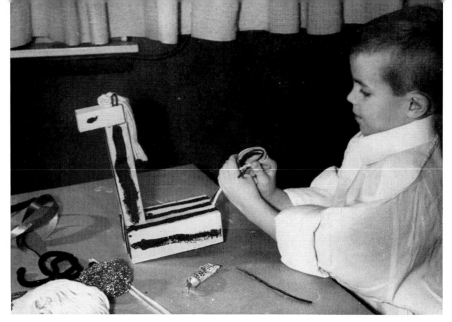

Yarn for a mane and pipe cleaners for ears and tail enhance the personality of this imaginary animal.

the animal and have developed—together—an original story, or stories, about possible adventures. The whole activity has so far been a truly creative experience.

But, someone asks, why can't each of them make an animal of his own which he could name and about which he could make up stories?

Well, why not? Our first problem will be getting the boxes. Does someone have suggestions how we might get them?

With this approach, do you think kindergartners will remember to look for boxes at home and be able to explain to Mother what all the boxes are for when she asks?

Here again we should keep in mind the basic purpose of our art activities. It isn't so much the final product that is important. Within a few weeks its importance will have faded in favor of some new experience. But the activity has presented many possibilities for solving new problems—problems which rely not upon a dictated solution, but rather upon original thinking on the part of each child. This stimulation of original, imaginative thinking and the resulting creative solution is the very heart of our program. This, indeed, is the primary justification of the time we spend on creative art activities in the home and in the classroom.

And how obvious it is that patterns, color books and Hectographed outlines never accomplish such goals.

Once our boxes have been securely attached to each other, there is the possibility of painting them. But the shiny glazed surface of some boxes resists the powder paint. So we add a bit of detergent to the paint which makes it stick successfully to the cardboard surfaces. And since the animals are imaginary or very free versions of real animals, we can use a playful approach in choosing colors to paint them.

Finally, some of the children may think of extra details which will give added life and vitality to their animals. Feathers, bits of ribbon or rope or buttons may be added if the children wish to do so. These, too, may be brought from home and kept in a special box of scrap materials.

Now your window sills are ready to become a veritable zoo from outer space. For many days imaginative stories and adventures will come rolling out of the children if they are given the opportunity and if they are made to feel that such activities are as important and as exciting to you as they are to them.

It is always the teacher, or the parent, who is the key to unlocking the doors of imaginative thinking and doing.

Wood Construction

MATERIALS:
work bench
basic tools
soft woods

Lucky is the youngster whose dad has some wood working tools and a spot in the garage or utility room where they may work together. Certainly every kindergarten room should be equipped with a work bench and a few basic tools because young children readily take to simple projects in wood construction.

The work bench should be about 24″ high with a thick top to permit pounding. A vise to hold wood for sawing and drilling should be attached to one corner of the bench.

A class of 24 children needs the following tools:

4 claw hammers, 8 oz.

3 small crosscut saws

1 wood file, 6″, half-round

6 coping saw frames

6 dozen 6″ loop-end coping saw blades

2 pairs of pliers

1 hand drill with set of twist drills

1 brace and set of auger bits

sandpaper, grades 0, ½ and 1

nails, variety of small sizes

1 counter brush and dust pan

Lumber yards usually are glad to give schools small scraps of wood and grocery stores often can provide wooden crates which can be knocked apart by parent or teacher. From such materials children can build their own versions of boats, trucks and trains. Sometimes, however, these scraps of wood (usually fir) are too hard for the young children to work with. Well-seasoned soft white pine or basswood are not cheap today, but they are much more suitable for the young child to work with if the budget permits their purchase. Boards ⅜″ to ½″ thick in a variety of widths (from 2″ to 8″) are ideal. Plywood is not suitable because the thin layers tend to split too easily.

Two-inch wooden wheels are a popular item. Children need them for cars, trucks and trains. They can be ordered through general school supply catalogs. Spools and wooden cores from paper rolls also may be added to the scrap box.

Four- and five-year-olds enjoy learning how to use tools so the work bench is a popular place for experimenting with original ideas. Simple versions of cars, trucks, boats and planes are favorite projects.

Photo: New York City Public Schools

Young children learn to place wood in a vise and that saw cuts on forward motion of pushing and pulling.

*With sandpaper wrapped around wood
block, child smoothes edges of wood.*

Children must be shown how to place wood in a vise for sawing. They must learn to saw fairly close to the vise to prevent vibration. It should be explained that the teeth of a saw are designed to cut on the *forward* motion and the weight of the saw does most of the work as we push, pull, push, pull.

The child learns that a hammer is held some distance from its head in order to give power to the swing. In choosing a nail, size is determined by the size of the pieces of wood to be joined. An over-sized nail will split a thin, narrow piece of wood.

A kindergartner enjoys using the hand drill and the brace and bit. Choose a soft piece of wood about ½″ thick and place it securely in the vise. The child will like the challenge of using a ¼″ drill. The punched board may not necessarily be used in a future construction. In fact, many of the child's first experiences in sawing, hammering and drilling are carried on for the pure pleasure of the physical activity. The child should be praised for these first steps in wood construction. If his efforts do not receive the approval of parent or teacher, he will not look forward to his turn at the work bench in the future.

"What a fine boat you have made," says the teacher to the youngster who has successfully nailed a small piece of wood on top of another, larger piece. "What color would you like to paint it?"

"Boats are usually named by their owners. What will you name your boat? How fine your boat will look in our display on the window sill."

A pat on the head is followed by other statements indicating approval and praise of the young child's first efforts. "What a fine worker you are, John. How proud your Mother and Dad will be when they see your boat."

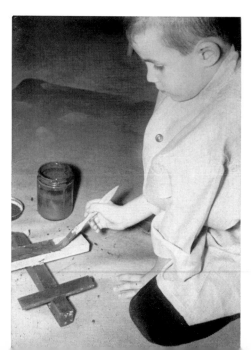

*When construction is completed, it may be
painted with tempera or powder paint.*

Stenciling

MATERIALS:
leaves
drawing paper
paint
screen wire about 8" x 10"
toothbrush

"It's Jimmy's and my turn. We're going to help each other today in stenciling. Look! I brought a whole bunch of pretty leaves and they are all different sizes like you said."

Young children can do beautiful stenciling and the activity provides many opportunities for learning to work together cooperatively.

The materials are inexpensive and easy to find. Fall leaves which the children pick up on their way to school are interesting shapes for first attempts. Sheets of drawing paper, powder paint, scraps of window screen wire and an old toothbrush are all that is necessary.

A single leaf can be placed in the center of the paper, or an arrangement of several leaves can be made. Two children hold the screen wire about 6" above the paper. A third youngster dips a toothbrush in powder paint, presses it against the inside of the jar to take off surplus paint which might drip, and then lightly brushes it across the screen wire. A fine mist of paint is thrown through the screen onto the paper below. Dark colored paint is recommended because, when the leaves are lifted from their places, the white silhouette shows up more dramatically against the dark background.

A toothbrush, screen wire and thinned poster paint are the necessary materials for stenciling. By lightly brushing the toothbrush across the screen wire a fine mist of color falls on the paper below.

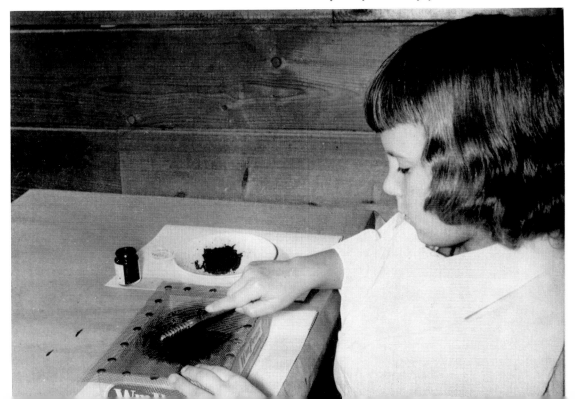

Dark colored paints show up best. Leaves of varying size and shape make a pleasing design.

Three children can work together successfully in this activity, two children assisting by holding the screen wire while a third works with the toothbrush. However, the flexibility of the screen wire makes it a bit awkward for young children to hold and we recommend mounting the screen wire to a sturdy fame. A wooden cigar box is the answer. By removing the top and knocking out the bottom, the screen wire can be tacked across the opening. Now a single child can easily hold the screen while a second child makes his stenciled design. Another advantage of this method is that the sides of the box form a natural guide for keeping the colored paint within a rectangular shape.

Plastic screen wire can be stretched between embroidery hoop frames for another one-man process.

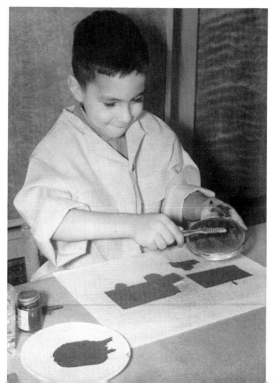

Another variation is the use of plastic screen wire which has been stretched between two parts of a round or oval embroidery hoop. Holding the hoop in one hand and brush in the other, a single child can move it over a larger surface than that covered by a cigar box.

After the children have experimented with leaves, they may cut shapes from construction paper such as animals, people, houses, trees and flowers. These may be placed on the paper to fill the space in a pleasing arrangement.

Remember, dark colors show up best. And be sure the paint is of fairly heavy consistency. Thin paint will cause heavy blobs of color. If the paint is too heavy it won't spatter properly. It should be explained to the children before they begin that the color should be built up slowly. We must not get in a hurry.

One group of kindergartners used full sheets of 12″ x 18″ manila paper. They printed on only one-half the sheet (9″ x 12″) so that the other half could be folded over like a cover. The finished prints were used as Christmas gifts for parents.

Monoprinting

MATERIALS:
tin cookie sheet
finger paint
newsprint paper, 12″ x 18″

Mono means *one.* So monoprinting is a process in which we make not many, but *one* print or design.

Then why not paint the idea directly on paper to begin with if we get only a single print or picture? Because printing techniques produce entirely different *textural* effects which cannot be achieved or duplicated through any other process. There are many exciting discoveries for the child to make as he sees his final design reversed on the printed surface. Monoprinting provides us with still another art process which helps the child stretch his creative imagination and encourages him to do original and inventive thinking.

One of the simplest processes for making a monoprint is through the use of finger paint, either the commercial or homemade variety.

Shiny cookie sheets provide an ideal surface upon which to work. It isn't necessary that we have as many cookie sheets as we have children. Eight or ten sheets will be sufficient and the children can take turns experimenting with this new activity. It is recommended that teachers purchase sheets about 10″ x 15″ in size, selecting sheets which have only one turned-up edge—usually along one end. Sheets which have more than one turned-up edge are not suitable for printing purposes.

First we spread a tablespoon of a dark colored finger paint over the cookie sheet with our hands until we have a smooth, opaque surface of color. Then we proceed just as if we were finger painting on paper. Using our fist, our thumbs, our forearms and outspread hands, we swish the color around, pressing hard so that the shiny surface of the cookie sheet can easily be seen. (See Finger Painting, page 41.)

When we have a design that pleases us, we wash our hands at the sink—quickly, so that the paint won't dry out.

Now we take a 12″ x 18″ sheet of unprinted newsprint paper and lay it carefully down on the surface of the paint. Don't get in a hurry. This should be done slowly so that the paper is centered over the design and there will be a margin of white all around. The teacher may demonstrate this once or twice and then—

Dark colored finger paint is spread evenly over the surface of a metal cookie sheet. Then the fist and side of hand are used to make design just as in finger painting.

hands off! The children should do their own printing and pulling of prints—even if they aren't quite straight.

With the palms of our hands we smooth the paper down so that all parts are brought into contact with the paint. We don't press too hard or the design will be pushed out of shape. We press just hard enough so that the paint will stick to the paper. Then starting with one end of the paper, we lift up—up—up. And behold, the paper has *lifted* the finger paint design right off the cookie sheet onto the paper. True, some of the paint still remains on the metal sheet, but not enough for another print. We will have to add more paint and make a new design for another monoprint.

Pulling the first print and seeing the design *in reverse* on the paper is an exciting event for everyone. Here the teacher will show her own excitement and enthusiasm which will carry over to her children and increase interest in the activity.

"Come see Martha's first print. She did it all by herself. Isn't it beautiful?"

"What a big, strong design David has made. And see how carefully he placed his paper over the sheet so that there is a white space all around his print. Good for you, David."

"When everyone has had a chance to make a print, we will have a big exhibition of our prints

After washing hands, a sheet of newsprint, slightly larger than cookie sheet, is lightly smoothed down over the painted surface.

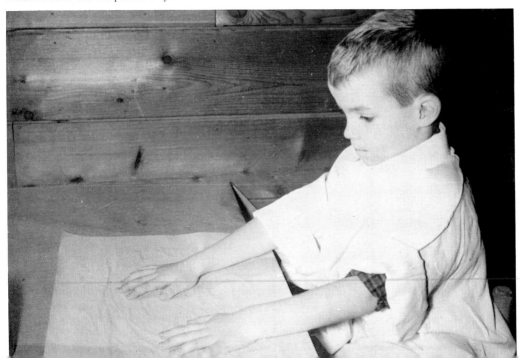

out in the hall for all the school to see. Won't everyone be surprised when they see our prints?"

Children will learn quickly that in printing processes the design on the finished print is *reversed* or backwards from the way they designed it on the original plate. If they make a tree on the left side of the cookie sheet, it will print on the right side of the paper. If they make some letters of the alphabet, they will be reproduced in reverse. This characteristic of the printing process can provide many interesting experiments for those children who become intrigued with this reverse technique. Of course, most of the designs will be abstract, non-realistic motions of the hand and fist which have no relationship to reality.

Because the paper itself is not wet as in the case of regular finger painting, our prints will not curl so badly. However, when they are entirely dry some may need to be pressed flat with a warm iron.

Prints will look even more effective when they are centered and stapled to 18″ x 24″ black construction paper. This will provide a handsome black border which will set off each print beautifully. Yes, it will take more space to display them properly, but the added satisfaction and personal pleasure the children get from seeing their work mounted and displayed will be worth the effort. There probably will not be room to display *all* the prints at one time in the classroom. But if a plan is worked out in advance *with the children*, a number of prints can be displayed each day until everyone is represented. Remember, we are not interested in displaying only the work of a choice few. Our objective is not to encourage only those who seem to achieve the neatest or most mature work. Our goal is to develop the creative potential in *all* our children. We are as interested in the creative development of one child as another. Therefore *all* the work is important and meaningful to us.

Carefully lifting one end, we see the design of our first monoprint.

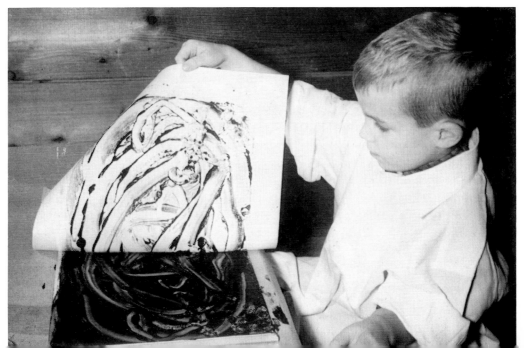

Vegetable Printing

MATERIALS:
vegetables
kitchen knife
paints and brushes
paper

"Come look at my carrot print."

"See, I'm using a radish to print with."

"Now I'm going to try a new design. I'll print my potato with red paint and then put the turnip in blue close to it."

These boys and girls are having an exciting new adventure printing with vegetables. Vegetable printing is easy to do and provides a new experience in learning about *repeat designs*. Here is how we might present the activity.

"Mary, what a beautiful design you have on your dress material. Won't you come to the front of the room so that everyone can see it? Look, boys and girls. See how the artist who designed Mary's dress material chose *this* interesting red shape and repeated it over and over and over—up and down and across the whole material. See how the red shape is repeated here—and here—and here.

"When a design idea is repeated all over a material like this we call it a *repeat design*. Let's say it together. *A repeat design*. Who else can find a repeat design on something he is wearing?

"John, will you come to the front of the room to show us your sport shirt? How many can see how the green and brown shapes are repeated over and over? What kind of a design do we call it? That's right. *A repeat design*.

"Did you know that we can learn to make our own repeat designs? Of course we can. And the big surprise is that we learn how to print our designs with *vegetables*—like radishes and carrots and potatoes."

Then the teacher—or Mother at home—can explain and demonstrate how repeat designs can be made and printed with vegetables.

We can use quite a wide variety of vegetables for our printing including potatoes, turnips, carrots and radishes. With a bit of imagination, some children will even experiment with leafy vegetables such as lettuce leaves. The uneven surface doesn't print a definite solid shape, but gives an interesting texture of color. These textures combine with the solid shapes to provide *variety* to our designs.

First the vegetables are washed and dried at the sink. Then with newspapers spread over a table or desk, we begin our experimentation in cutting the vegetables with a kitchen paring knife.

In the classroom, it is recommended that a work table be used for the cutting part of the activity. The teacher demonstrates how this is done, explaining carefully to the class how to hold the vegetable, the knife, and the importance of getting a smooth, direct cut clear across the vegetable at one stroke. If the surface is ragged or uneven, we explain, it won't print well.

Let's say that we are demonstrating how to cut a carrot for printing. We show the children how we place it down on the table surface. With one hand we hold the vegetable near one end to keep it steady. The other hand holds the knife. Then, with a good firm stroke, we cut straight across the carrot. This may be near the middle, or if we want a very small shape to print, down near the small end. At this age level, we do not recommend attempting to cut a design *into* the surface of the vegetable, but use the total surface as the printing shape. Variety will come through size and color.

Later, when the children are ready to do their own cutting, they can take turns coming to the cutting table in groups of five or six. With careful supervision, there is no reason why kindergartners can't do their own cutting.

They should learn how to use a knife properly.

For the printing, the teacher chooses a jar of powder paint and with a brush, paints the end of the carrot. Then, pressing slowly and firmly, she prints it on a sheet of paper. This isn't a quick *stamp*, but a slow, firm pressure on the paper. The carrot is then painted again and printed a second time. We point out that the carrot must be painted *each time it is printed*. We do not try to print five or six times with just one painting.

The important goals in this activity for young children are the experimentation with different shapes, learning to apply the right amount of paint (too little makes a weak print and too much makes a splotch) and discovering the joy and satisfaction of printing the shapes. We are not too concerned at this age level with how neatly and accurately spaced the child can produce a repeat design.

The teacher, in her demonstration, lets the children observe her interest and enthusiasm for *experimenting* with the different shapes and colors. For example, she may print a carrot shape in red several times, then try a potato shape in blue or green or black. When one shape of color has dried, she may even experiment with over-lapping colored shapes. It is important that she *not* try to produce a finished looking product. Her job is to stimulate the children by her own excitement with the many possibilities for *experimentation*. This is as far as she should go at this time. If she has done her job well, the children are eager to start experimentation on their own.

Perhaps it is well to stop for a moment and point out that teachers and parents should not fear that this type of demonstration will limit or retard the creative expression of young children. We are not demonstrating or dictating what the *final product* will look like. That is determined in the creative act itself which must be an individual experience for each child. What we *are* demonstrating is the *process* of using materials. These are the tools—the language—of creative expression. Obviously we would not give a child a whole potato, a knife, paint and paper and merely say, "Now express yourself." The child needs guidance in the use of materials, tools and processes. That is the role of the parent and teacher. What the child does with these is the *creative experience*.

Using a scrap of wood as a cutting board and holding the vegetable back from the knife blade, we learn to make a clean, straight cut.

*First we experiment to see how well our shapes print.
Loading a brush with paint, we carefully brush across
the freshly cut end of the vegetable and firmly press it
down on the paper.*

After the children have had an opportunity to print their vegetables at random, the teacher might refer back to examples of repeat designs on clothing fabrics. Here she points out how an idea—a design—is repeated over and over. To demonstrate this, she might print a row across the top of a sheet of paper, spacing the prints several inches apart. Then she prints a second row several inches below the first. Then a third row and so on, depending upon the size of the paper. But she will not try to be too exact in her spacing since she is not attempting to set up an adult standard of achievement, but rather *explain a principle of repetition.*

And now the children are ready to experiment with the idea of a consciously repeated design. And here we will keep in mind that some of our young children may not be sufficiently mature to grasp this idea. That is quite all right. Our objective has been merely to open a door, to show a direction for those who are ready for this step. For those who are not ready for this type of conscious planning the activity must still be a happy and satisfying one.

Each child works according to his own capacity and ability. We enjoy and compliment each for his individual achievement. One is not "better" than another. In the creative experience, we are concerned with *individual development.* If we really believe in providing for individual differences, we must put this belief into action in our program of art activities.

Vegetable printing, like other activities suggested in this book, may be repeated several times during the year. It will be helpful to see how the children grow in their abilities to handle tools, to control paint and begin to develop design concepts.

Our objective is to provide experiences which will expand their horizons of understanding and manipulative skills. But, most important of all, we are developing the creative potential which we know exists within each one of our children.

Now we are ready to make a repeat design. First we print one shape in one color for several rows. Then we choose another shape and a second color to add to our design. No matter that the lines are not straight. We are enjoying an activity which does not require the accuracy and precision of a machine.

Found Objects

MATERIALS:
Children search for
beautiful objects in
nature—found objects

This is an experience in art appreciation—the appreciation of beautiful objects that can be found in nature.

It is easy to overlook the wonders of nature and to dismiss them as being just ordinary. Nature is always with us, so we tend to take it for granted. But is it not important for children—even very young children—to become aware of nature and the beautiful things it creates? Such an awareness gives us a deeper appreciation for the world we live in and a new respect for the mysteries of the universe.

Children of kindergarten age are ready for this experience, but they need the stimulation of an adult who loves nature and can become excited about the beauty which can be found in the simplest objects. A teacher needs only to stop on the way to school to pick up a few leaves in the fall or a budding branch in the spring to create an interest which will soon have the classroom overflowing with exciting objects which children are really *seeing* for the first time.

"Look, boys and girls. On the way to school this morning I looked down on the ground to see what I could find that was truly beautiful. See what I found. Look at these leaves. What beautiful shapes they have. Here is one with points which seem to flow in and out, in and out. Let's turn it over. See the delicate veins on the back? And what beautiful colors. See how the reds and browns blend into each other. There are so many, many leaves all around us that sometimes we don't stop to look at how beautiful they really are.

"Here is a rock I found that I like very much. John, come hold my rock in your hand. Feel how smooth it is. There aren't any rough places at all. Do you suppose it has been smoothed down by years and years of rain and just rolling around on the ground?

Even very young children become fascinated with texture and can enjoy the wonders of nature—if these things are called to their attention. Gibson asks Rosie to feel the rough texture of the piece of tree bark he found while Megan feels the smooth surface of a stone.

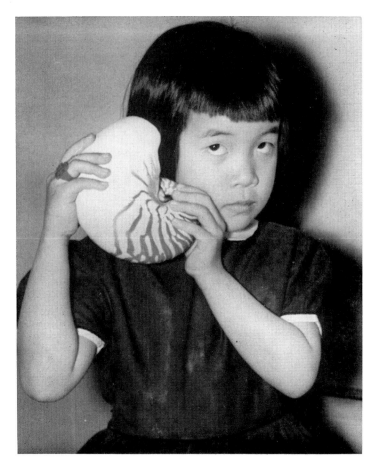

"And here is a shell that I found last summer at the beach. See how it twists itself around into a shape like a curl. The outside of the shell is all white, but look at the beautiful colors on the inside. See how the ribs make lines that follow the curving shape. Marilyn, would you like to hold my shell and *feel* its shape? Put it close to your ear and listen. Do you hear a roaring sound? They say that is the roar of the sea you hear. Of course it isn't true, but isn't it nice to imagine that it really is the sea?

"As you walk back and forth from school, look carefully to see what you can find that is beautiful to look at and interesting to touch and feel. Maybe it will be a bit of rough bark from a tree. Perhaps you will find a pretty stone or even a stick that has an unusual shape. Bring the things you find to school and we will put them on a special table where everyone can enjoy them with you. We will call them our *found objects* because *we* found them."

What do we do with all the things children find that they think are beautiful? We enjoy them with the children. We exclaim over their ability to find unusual objects and are delighted that they can enjoy them as we do.

Enjoying nature is not an activity which we participate in for only a week or two during the year. This awareness of natural beauty is something we want to instill deep within the hearts of our boys and girls so that it will always remain a part of them.

But first we must have this awareness ourselves. First we must respond to nature and see and feel its beauty deeply within ourselves. Then we must have the courage to express our feelings to the children we teach so that our excitement is transferred to them and stimulates them to respond instinctively and naturally to all that is beautiful about them. This is the way we develop young people who are sensitive to beauty and who, throughout their lives, will respond to the wonders of nature.

Collage:
A Design to Feel

MATERIALS:
shirt cardboard
items from scrap box
paste

Here is a new word for young children to learn. *Collage* means to paste down or attach. So a collage is a design in which various objects are attached to a surface in an arrangement that is pleasing to the eye. And because we will be emphasizing *texture* as a new element from which we can derive pleasure, we will add the additional factor of *touch*. Yes, we are going to make a design which we can actually *feel* and enjoy with our hands as well as our eyes.

Such a design does not have to be related to reality. It will not represent *something*. It will be intriguing to the eye and the sense of touch purely because of its interesting lines, colors, shapes and textures. Most collages are therefore *abstract* designs. And even very young children delight in making them.

The materials we will use are easily available. First we need a supply of shirt cardboards which the children can bring from home. This provides a good surface upon which to make our collages. Then we will go to our well-stocked box of scrap materials and select a number of relatively flat items such as bits of cloth, feathers, ribbons, decorative papers, cotton and even sandpaper. To attach these to the cardboard each child will need a small container of paste.

How shall we present this activity to young children? Here, again, the parent or teacher can make good use of a demonstration.

The purpose of our demonstration will be two-fold. First we want to stimulate the child's interest and awareness in the *feel* of different textures. Second, we want him to enjoy the adventure of choosing a number of different surfaces and arranging them into a design.

A collage is planned using a wide variety of textured materials: scraps of silk, sandpaper, feathers, ribbons and dozens of other things from the scrap box. Then it is all pasted down on a shirt cardboard.

For our demonstration let us choose a group of six or seven items which have quite different textures. For example, we might select a bit of silk or satin, a piece of leather from an old glove or shoe, a feather, a piece of bark from a tree, perhaps some screen wire and a sheet of sandpaper. We talk about these to the children, closing our eyes while we feel one or two and try to describe how they feel to us. Then we might ask for several volunteers who will close their eyes and be given one of the objects. Can they tell what it is just by touching it? Does it feel soft or hard? Rough or smooth? Does everything have its own special feel? Feel a wool sweater, the surface of our wooden desks, the chalkboard, the plastered walls of the classroom. Each has its own texture. And while all of them do not necessarily feel *pleasant* to the touch, the *process of feeling* the surface is an interesting and enjoyable experience.

Having created an interest in this new sense of touch, we continue our demonstration by arranging a group of these items on a shirt card-board. With our scissors we cut and redesign the shape of certain items so that some will be large, some middle-sized and some quite small. This differentness in size, we point out, is a good way to help make our designs more interesting. And we can remember it by thinking of the story of the three bears in which there was a big papa bear, a middle-sized mama bear and a little baby bear.

In cutting the shapes, however, we will not try to make them represent anything recognizable. They may be just squares or long rectangles or oval shapes. Such items as feathers and bits of wood bark we will leave in their original shapes.

After pushing the items around, talking about how we want them to fill the space—rather than all be pushed down in one corner or on one side of the cardboard—we are ready to paste. But by now the children are eager to experiment on their own. So we won't hold up their progress any longer.

When the children's collages are completed, they may be displayed on a bulletin board or in the hall corridor. Each might be placed on a 12″ x 18″ sheet of colored construction paper selected by the child. The explanatory note can read, "Come *feel* our collages." You won't have to wait long for children and adults to pay your exhibit a visit. Your "designs for feeling" are an assured success.

Anyone can make a design to see. How much more interesting to make one to see and feel!

Photo: Chicago Public Schools

Halloween

MATERIALS:
paper sacks
scissors
paints
colored papers
paste

"I'm going to dress up like a ghost for Halloween and I'll scare everybody in the room."

"See the funny mask I made. No one will know who I am."

"Can we have a Halloween parade so everyone can see us all dressed up?"

Ghosts, goblins and witches become important topics for conversation as October 31 draws near. And what fine opportunities they present for developing imaginative thinking.

Although children will bring commercially made masks to school to show their classmates, we can stimulate interest in making their own by planning a special Halloween party or parade in which each youngster will be expected to wear a mask which he has designed and made for himself.

Probably the simplest mask to make is one from a large grocery sack. This should be one which is just big enough to slip over the head easily. By cutting off four or five inches, the open end of the sack will rest on the shoulders and the closed end touches the top of the head.

With the sack placed correctly on the head, each child can feel with his finger where his eyes are located and will indicate their position by marking them with a wax crayon. These marks will serve as a guide for cutting holes for eyes. After the marks are made, the sack is removed from the head and scissors are used to cut the openings. They can be round or oval or even square. There is no one right way. Each child will have his own ideas on the subject.

Now the sack is ready to be decorated. Crayons do not show up well on brown paper, so we will use either paint or pieces of colored construction paper pasted to the surface of the

Indispensable man in October is Mr. Jack-O-Lantern. Making him is a little messy but even smell is part of Halloween.

Pumpkins play a role in painting activities as well as witches, cats and other symbols of the season.

sack. And, of course, there is always the box of scrap materials where such items as feathers, cotton and bits of ribbon will often give just the right touch that is needed.

In this activity the children should be encouraged to let their imaginations go completely free. Almost anything goes.

Jim has decided to paint his mask. He chooses black and white with a touch of bright red. Doris wants to use green and brown paint. Randy prefers to cut out pieces of colored paper and paste them on. He chooses blue, purple and light gray.

Marie decides that she wants some long ears on her mask so she cuts them from a shirt cardboard and paints them with powder paint. But

Most exciting is the making of masks. These kindergartners are using large grocery sacks and are decorating them with paint and bits of colored paper.

she has trouble in deciding how to attach them. Here is where Mother or teacher can help with a stapling machine.

When all the masks are completed the children take turns trying them on and parading around the room for all to see. What a fine party we are going to have!

Making a real pumpkin head is a cooperative project which several children can work on together. The teacher will need to do the preliminary cutting, but the children can dig out the inside and draw with a crayon where they think the eyes, nose and mouth should be located.

Halloween also calls for paintings of witches and black cats and ghosts and pumpkin heads. Large sheets of black paper on which to paint provide an appropriate seasonal feeling.

Halloween puppets made of paper sacks (see page 36) can also stimulate the development of original stories. Here is another opportunity for effective dramatic productions which will appeal to even the most timid youngster.

The classroom parade is an exciting event. Small matter that a child is lucky if he finds he can see through only one eye-hole of his mask.

Thanksgiving

MATERIALS:
paint
brushes
paper

What does Thanksgiving mean to a very young child? Can a Pilgrim become a meaningful concept to him? Is he able to understand the contributions made by our forefathers? Probably not. Then what should we do about this important holiday and how can we involve young children in creative experiences which are related to it?

Perhaps we should take our cue from the purpose of the first Thanksgiving. We are told that the Pilgrim Fathers, with Indians as their guests, celebrated and gave thanks for their first American harvest. They gathered about tables loaded with game and fish, wild fruits from the forest, and corn bread and vegetables from their new gardens. This was in

What is Thanksgiving without the traditional turkey? But there is no place for stereotyped patterns. How much more exciting is the child's personal expression of a turkey—as he sees it and knows it to be.

Even a very young child can be taught to be thankful for what he has. When Rickie was asked what he was thankful for, he constructed his own version of the new home his family recently purchased.

October of 1621, the first autumn of the exiles in their new home.

Instead of attempting to build our art experiences around historical facts which are beyond the understanding of young children, let us use Thanksgiving as a time for becoming aware of the many things for which we ourselves can be thankful. Obviously, a young child has little basis for understanding and comparing his relative good fortune with that of other children in the world. However, without delving too deeply into unfortunate conditions under which many children live today, it can be pointed out that there are many children in the world who do not have the nice homes we live in, the good food and even the many toys which most of us have.

But let's go beyond being thankful for material things. Here is an opportunity to become more aware and grateful for a family who loves us, of friends who enjoy being with us, of the pleasures of coming to school and the many things we learn there. And, perhaps most important of all in our celebration of a day of thanksgiving, we can talk together about how we can show and express our thankfulness by doing things for others. After all is this not the proof of our thankfulness?

Now we can see how absurd it would be to spend time tracing around a pattern of a Pilgrim or a turkey. Such activities are not meaningful experiences to children and are only busy work which adults have invented for bored children.

How much more meaningful it will be for our children to paint a picture about something for which they are truly thankful, or to model in clay—no matter how simple a symbol it may be—a member of their family or a friend they love. Perhaps even more than Christmas—which often emphasizes receiving rather than giving—Thanksgiving might become a time for *giving*—of oneself, of something we have made to someone we love or care for deeply.

Thanksgiving can provide an opportunity for us to emphasize the *human values* in living and to put thankfulness into positive action.

Ronnie was thankful for the big yard he plays in and painted a picture of it with him raking the leaves.

Christmas

MATERIALS:
paints
brushes
paper
items from scrap box for
    Christmas ornaments

Of all the holiday seasons, Christmas is perhaps the most exciting for young children. From the moment the tree is brought into the room until cleanup after the last-day-of-school Christmas party, kindergartners are eager to participate in art activities which involve the Spirit of Christmas.

Holly and bells and candles are age-old symbols. But the kindergarten teacher will not be satisfied merely to follow traditions of the past. She will seek out ideas that stimulate and develop the creativeness which she knows exists in each of her children. This is no time for stale patterns of Santas, candles and candy canes.

Of course, the Christmas Story will be told and retold to the children providing inspiration for many art activities. The children will want to make ornaments for the trees, gifts for their parents and paintings which show their understanding of the meaning of Christmas.

Easels should be kept well stocked with paints, brushes and large sheets of paper. In fact, we can add new interest to our painting activities by providing several colors not previously available to the children. For instance, try adding a jar of pink or red-violet or yellow-orange. Call the attention of the children to

What is it? The five-year-old looks you squarely in the eye and says, "It is a design and I'm going to hang it on the Christmas tree. I made it with wire and paper and dipped it in plaster and then sprinkled red glitter all over."

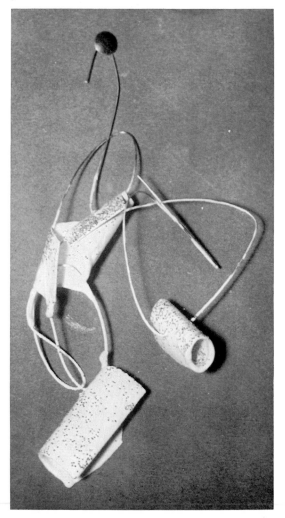

Each child makes his own original Christmas tree ornaments to give a festive look to the kindergarten room for the holiday season.

these new colors. Where can they use them in their paintings?

"Come look at my painting. I made the Baby Jesus pink all over."

"I used the new red-violet color on one of my Wise Men. Now he looks just like a king."

"Look at Ronnie's painting, boys and girls. He painted a star that glows in the sky with the new yellow-orange. And see how he echoed the same color in other parts of his picture."

Perhaps some child will bring a crèche to school. It may be a prized possession which

has long been in the family or an inexpensive one of cardboard from the five-and-ten. The children will love the little figures and arrange and rearrange them on the table. But this should prove only an inspiration to making a crèche of their own. The figures might be made of clay or papier-mâché pulp, or perhaps paper and lightweight cardboard.

Eager hands will search the scrap box for bits of bright colored cloth, yarn, felt and paper to make original Christmas tree ornaments. If we purchase a few packages of glitter and se-

A cardboard tube, tissue paper and bright spots of pink paint were the ingredients for this charming Christmas tree nagel. A pipe cleaner was used as a "hanger."

*Santa's head was built around an oatmeal box
covered with white construction paper and
painted with bright colored powder paints.*

quins the children will enjoy spreading a bit of paste on some parts of their work to sprinkle with glitter or carefully add a sequin here and there.

What to make as gifts for Mother and Dad? If we really believe in a program of creative experiences, this is no time to bring out a step-by-step project for every child to make according to instructions. Many so-called "useful" gifts for parents made by kindergartners are impractical and seldom used. How much better for the child to give something he has made during the year which is really his own. In might be a drawing or one of his rich-colored paintings carefully rolled in tissue and tied with a bright colored ribbon. It will be prized as highly as an awkward looking ash try or book end which does not function well. A simple pinch pot made of clay or a piece of fruit formed of papier-mâché pulp will be gratefully received. In any case, the *creative* experience in art is especially appropriate at this time.

*This shining white angel was painted by a four-year-old
on deep blue paper to represent the angel who kept
watch at night over the baby Jesus.*

Easter

MATERIALS:
eggs
water-color brushes
paints

Many of our Easter customs involving the use of colored eggs and rabbits date back to ancient times and are symbols of new life. Easter is a joyous festival of spring which lends itself to many activities in which young children may participate.

Coloring Easter eggs tops the list of favorite Easter activities. Children can bring hard-boiled eggs from home and decorate them with their own original designs. For this purpose we use small water-color brushes and tempera or poster paint. No restrictions in color here—we encourage the children to experiment freely with a wide range of colors.

We should remember, however, that the children have been painting *big* on large sheets of paper. Painting a design on an egg is a sudden change in scale. So we talk together about making small designs for small things like eggs, instead of big designs which we made to fill up big sheets of paper. We discover together how the small brush can make little dots, dashes,

circles and many other small shapes. In fact, it is a good idea for the children to invent some small designs on paper with their brushes before painting directly on the eggs.

Most young children will respond immediately to the idea and find real pleasure in working on the new, small scale. However, some will not be ready for such details. But we have set no specific standards. We will not be overly concerned about those whose muscular coordination does not permit such control. We will not make them feel uncomfortable or that their work is not acceptable. We will enjoy their big, bold masses of color and will tell them so.

How about an Easter egg tree? A tree branch, stuck in a large pot of sand, makes a wonderful egg tree. This can be hung with real eggs whose contents have been blown out after piercing the ends with an ice pick. The eggs can be dipped in commercial Easter egg dye. Or eggs can be cut from colored construction

Using a small brush and tempera paints, Tom paints designs on hard-boiled eggs for Easter.

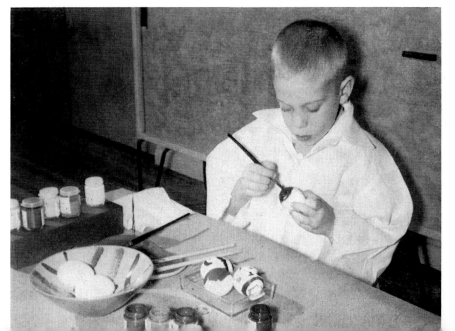

paper and decorated by pasting on bits of colored papers. Still another possibility is making eggs from scraps of printed fabric. Children cut out two roundish shapes (no patterns, please), put a bit of cotton between them, and sew them together to make a three-dimensional version of an egg.

If some youngster owns a rabbit, perhaps he can bring it to school for a day or two. Here is a splendid opportunity for direct observation prior to modeling the pet in clay or making paintings. Talk about the shape of the rabbit. Encourage the children to describe its ears, the shape of the head, body, legs and tail. Encourage the children to draw the rabbit in the air with their hands. Draw him *big*—even bigger than he really is. Draw him on the chalkboard. Make a game of painting pictures which show the rabbit *doing* things—eating, running, jumping. In this way, each child is

An Easter egg tree is almost as exciting as a Christmas tree, especially when the eggs are brightly patterned bits of fabric stuffed with cotton and sewed by young hands.

*According to this kindergartner, the Easter angel—
like the Christmas angel—hovers over us to see that
everything is all right.*

stimulated to draw, paint and model what he
personally understands and knows about the
animal.

For an Easter project, a kindergarten class in
Detroit stuffed grocery sacks with old newspapers and twisted them into shapes of hens
and roosters. Wings, tail feathers and wattles
were made of colored construction paper and
pasted on. For several days the local "hen
house" was a favorite gathering spot for the
children and their friends.

In Cincinnati, a group of kindergartners
designed and colored huge paper eggs which
they pinned to a giant paper-painted tree.
Some of the children were able to understand
the idea of *border designs* and invented some of
their own to color across the paper eggs. Others,
not so advanced in their drawing, were happy
to fill the space with wandering lines of color.
Each was praised for his efforts and was assured
a place for his contribution on the giant Easter
egg tree.

*Here is a convincing chicken house with hens laying
eggs—Easter eggs, of course—by the dozen.*

Photo: Detroit Public Schools

May Day

MATERIALS:
small containers
paints
colored papers
paste

If Easter celebrates the coming of spring, May Day is a joyous festival announcing the coming of summer. Spring rains and the warm sun make it possible for nature to come alive again. Trees are wrapped in new coats of green, neat rows of vegetable gardens make geometric patterns in our back yards and, best of all, flowers are blooming in wild riots of color.

Indeed, flowers are the symbol of May Day, and the making of May baskets and other types of containers for bouquets is a favored activity with young children.

But let's keep the experience an original one which calls for creative thinking and problem solving. Parents and teachers should not rely upon stereotyped patterns for May baskets with each child following identical instructions so that their work looks alike. Instead, we will provide a variety of materials and the stimula-

tion and guidance which results in each child developing containers reflecting his own thinking and planning.

For this we provide quite a variety of materials. Very few young children can make an actual container without considerable help from an adult. Therefore it is recommended that we provide a collection of basic shapes as foundations upon which the children can build. These might include paper cups, milk cartons, cardboard containers for cottage cheese and tin cans. How these containers are decorated becomes the creative problem-solving art activity with each child arriving at a different and unique solution.

Powder paint, with detergent added, will adhere to waxy or metallic surfaces. The painting of the containers might include, first, a solid coat of color. Then when this has dried, a con-

May day calls for May baskets, so we begin early to make a collection of tin cans, paper cups, milk cartons and other containers that will hold water.

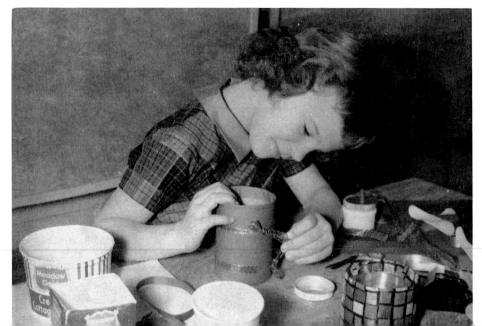

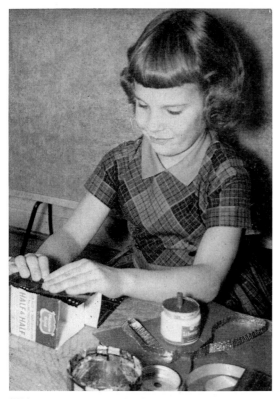

With an assortment of colored construction papers, decorative Christmas wrappings and bits of ribbon, Kim decorates the containers according to her own ideas.

Selecting flowers that are suitable for each container takes a bit of experimenting and some careful planning. We cut the stems so that some stand high in the middle and others fill in around the edges.

trasting color or two can be used to add decorative designs. For these designs, medium sized water-color brushes are used.

Colored construction papers may also be used to cover containers. Because it is difficult to make paste stick to these surfaces, it is recommended that the children cut strips of colored paper sufficiently long that they will wrap around the container at least one and a half times. In this way the paper will be pasted to paper instead of directly to the container. Decorative stripes or other shapes of contrasting colors may be pasted on the surface.

We need not limit our May Day activities to the making of flower containers. There are other activities which can use flowers as a basic motif.

Using 12″ x 18″ sheets of manila paper as backgrounds, children can cut flowers including stems and leaves from colored construction papers and paste them down for a cutting and pasting activity.

For an interesting variation of a painting activity, provide 18″ x 24″ black construction paper on which children may paint imaginary bouquets of flowers. Be sure that the paint is thick enough to be opaque. Then enjoy with the children how brilliantly the colors show up against the black background.

Still another possibility is to set aside a section of the chalkboard where each child may "paint" some flowers with colored chalks. Perhaps for a day or two the entire chalkboard can blossom out with gay drawings of "signs of summer."